100 RANDOM VILLAGES IN THE UK

The rich history it's easy to overlook

by Ryan Wakeman

Contents

Bibury

Nestled amongst the rolling hills of the Cotswolds, Bibury welcomes visitors to explore its quaint and charming village. It's easy to see why Bibury has been a favourite destination for centuries, with its picturesque scenery and rich history that is still evident in the architecture and surroundings. Here's what you need to know about Bibury:

Bibury boasts a fascinating past that can be traced back to the ancient Roman era. It was founded in the 7th century and became a thriving market town in the Middle Ages, with wool production being the primary source of income. In the 16th century, wealthy wool merchants built grand country houses in the area, adding to the unique charm that Bibury is known for.

One notable figure in Bibury's history is William Morris, a prominent textile designer, artist, and writer who resided in the village between 1890 and 1896. Bibury still cherishes his legacy today, with visitors able to tour Morris's home, Kelmscott Manor, which has been preserved in its original form. The village also contains the Church of St. Mary's, built in the 12th century, and other historically significant structures.

Perhaps Bibury's most recognizable landmark is Arlington Row, a collection of stone cottages dating back to the 17th century. The cottages embody the traditional Cotswolds architectural style and are among the most photographed in the country. Bibury Trout Farm, operational for over a century, offers guests the rare opportunity to catch their own trout from the River Coln.

Despite its village status, Bibury boasts an array of traditions and cultural activities. For instance, Bibury Silver Band, founded in the late 19th century, continues to perform at local events and festivals; an annual duck race sets 1,500 plastic ducks afloat on the River Coln and includes prizes for the fastest ducks; and Bibury's thriving art community houses several galleries showcasing the work of local artists. The River Coln itself provides the perfect backdrop for walking trails and hiking paths surrounded by the rolling hills and meadows.

With a small but lively community and maintaining its charm and authenticity, Bibury remains a popular destination for tourists and locals alike. The village boasts a selection of local businesses, such as traditional teahouses, antique shops, and pubs, that contribute to its character. Bibury also hosts regular events and activities that foster a strong sense of community spirit among residents.

Castle Combe

Nestled in the heart of Wiltshire's stunning countryside lies the picturesque village of Castle Combe. With its historic architecture, lush green surroundings and unique charm, it's no surprise that it has captured the hearts of tourists and filmmakers alike. This quintessential English village offers a glimpse into a bygone era, where visitors can immerse themselves in the enduring spirit of English country life.

The village boasts a rich history that dates back to the Roman period, with its heyday during the Middle Ages when it served as a bustling market town and wool-trading centre. Its historic legacy is still visible today through iconic buildings like the medieval market cross, the 14th-century St. Andrew's church, and the 15th-century castle keep.

Castle Combe's visual appeal has also attracted filmmakers, with notable appearances in films such as War Horse and Stardust. It's easy to see why; the village's honey-colored houses made of local stone, adorned with flower boxes and old-fashioned signs, give a warm and inviting feel. The village also features quaint shops, cafes, and pubs that offer traditional English fare that will surely delight visitors.

The village's bustling community holds a strong sense of pride in their heritage, cultivating a robust sense of community spirit. In addition to annual village fetes and Christmas markets, the village has an active arts scene, with exhibitions and workshops regularly held at the village hall. Castle Combe also boasts a primary school, village shop, and even a race track, which has hosted high-profile motorsport events year after year.

With rolling hills, meadows, and woodlands surrounding the village, Castle Combe's natural features add to its timeless appeal. The village is a haven for outdoor activities and sports, especially with the Castle Combe Circuit being a famous race track that hosts several high-profile motorsport events each year.

Castle Combe is more than just a pretty picture; it combines a rich history, cultural heritage, and natural beauty, offering visitors a chance to experience the enduring charm of English country life. Whether it's a getaway from the hustle and bustle of modern life or an adventure into history and culture, Castle Combe is a destination that visitors will undoubtedly cherish.

Lacock

Nestled in the idyllic Wiltshire countryside lies the charming village of Lacock, a place steeped in history and overflowing with character. Its most notable landmark is the breathtaking Lacock Abbey, an awe-inspiring Gothic structure that has captured the hearts and imaginations of visitors from all over the world. But there's much more to this quaint village than simply a photo op – Lacock's connection to the history of photography is both significant and fascinating.

Dating back to the 13th century, Lacock's roots can be traced back to the Abbey of Shaftesbury. In the 16th century, it was passed onto the Thynne family of Longleat and remained in their hands until the 1940s. Take a stroll through the village, and you'll feel transported back in time, with quintessentially English architecture and preserved buildings at every turn. One of Lacock's most notable residents was William Henry Fox Talbot, a pioneer of photography.

Lacock Abbey was founded in 1232 and boasts an impressive history. In the 19th century, William Henry Fox Talbot used the Abbey's south gallery as his photographic studio, where he developed the "calotype" process, an early photographic printing technique. Alongside the Abbey, stands the village's 14th Century Tithe Barn, a National Trust venue now used for hosting weddings and concerts.

Though small in size, Lacock has an indomitable community spirit. Annual events include a Christmas Fayre, summer Open Gardens event, and the Lacock at War event, which celebrates the village's connection to the military. Surrounded by rolling fields and the gentle River Avon, Lacock is an oasis of natural beauty.

Today, Lacock is a haven for tourists from around the globe, who come to see the village and Abbey. Visitors can experience local pubs, cafes, and shops – a perfect way to unwind. The village has also maintained its strong connection to photography, with various events and exhibitions. Many artists call Lacock home, making it a hub of creativity and inspiration. Furthermore, it is a popular filming location for TV and movies.

In conclusion, Lacock is a village with a rich history, plenty of culture, and exquisite natural surroundings. Its connection to the history of photography is a fascinating aspect worth exploring. But it is also a charming place to visit or live, with a strong sense of community, heritage, and natural beauty. Exploring Lacock is a journey through time, and a celebration of England's beautiful architecture, culture, and scenic splendor.

Clovelly

Discovering the Fascinating History and Unique Charms of Clovelly
Nestled on the stunning North Devon coast lies the captivating village of
Clovelly, renowned for its car-free streets and rich fishing heritage. The
village's traditional buildings and cobbled pathways will transport you back in
time. This article delves into the history of Clovelly, its cultural attractions,
and modern-day appeal.

For over a thousand years, Clovelly has seen a lot of changes. Owned by the
Giffard family for centuries, the village became a hub for fishing in the 1200s,
with fishermen selling their catch in major cities like London. However, the fish
began to dwindle in the eighteenth century, causing prosperity to dwindle as
well.

Clovelly has been home to many events and notable individuals over the
centuries. The village was a haven for smugglers during the eighteenth and
nineteenth centuries, with infamous names like Thomas Benson and Stephen
Boswell running operations. Additionally, Charles Kingsley, the renowned
Victorian author of "Westward Ho!" was born here.

Clovelly's most iconic feature is its steep, car-free streets, where donkeys
transport goods up and down. Visitors can also explore the Court Gardens,
which date back to the early 18th century and offer stunning views of the
Bristol Channel and rare plant species. The harbor, in use since the medieval
era, still houses a small fishing fleet and fish quay where visitors can glimpse
and savor the freshest seafood.

Clovelly's character is not only found in its quaint streets and traditional
landmarks. The village is famous for its close-knit community spirit, as
demonstrated through its annual festivals. The Clovelly Lobster and Crab
Feast in September celebrates the village's fishing heritage, while the non-
profit Clovelly Herring Festival in November is a food lover's paradise.

Clovelly's community is supported by independent shops and small eateries,
including craft stores showcasing handmade jewelry and knitwear, as well as
sweet shops selling traditional confections. These establishments are all
proudly locally owned.

Clovelly's stunning natural surroundings and landscape features are truly
breathtaking. Visitors can explore the many coastal paths, hiking or cycling
through the countryside. The South West Coast Path is a must-visit, providing
panoramic views of towering cliffs and the Bristol Channel.
rediscovered.

Polperro

Nestled on the southern coast of Cornwall, Polperro is a delightful fishing village close to the bustling towns of Looe and Fowey. With its charming cobbled streets, quaint cottages, and rugged coastline, Polperro is a picturesque location brimming with history and character.

From its Bronze Age origins to its infamous smuggling past in the 16th and 17th centuries, Polperro has a rich history that has left its imprint on the village. The narrow streets, twisting alleys, and hidden tunnels once provided the perfect cover for illegal trades in Dutch gin, French brandy, and tobacco. The Trelawny family, among the village's most notorious smugglers, were instrumental in these operations. Later, the village shifted its focus to fishing, thriving on herring and pilchard from the sea.

The Polperro Heritage Museum, located in the heart of the village, offers insight into the area's cultural character. It tells tales of its smuggling and fishing stories to its resident artists and writers such as Stephen Macey and Mary Fletcher. The Polperro Model Village is a fantastic replica of the village's historic charm, and the harbour is one of the village's focal points.

The annual Polperro Festival celebrating music, art, dance, and storytelling is an event not to be missed, with visitors and locals alike flocking to the streets for a week of festivities and entertainment. The village also has a thriving arts and crafts community, with independent galleries scattered about.

Polperro's rugged coastline with its towering cliffs and secluded coves is awe-inspiring. The South West Coast Path spanning 630 miles from Minehead to Poole offers stunning views of the Atlantic. Scenic trails through the village are ideal for hiking, offering sweeping views of the landscape.

The village's dining scene is excellent, with cosy and elegant restaurants serving a range of cuisines. Independent shops offer unique artisanal goods, from handmade jewellery to delicious homemade fudge.

All in all, Polperro is an ideal destination for anyone seeking to discover the history, culture, and natural beauty of southern Cornwall. With something for everyone, it's an indispensable part of any UK traveller's itinerary.

Port Isaac

Nestled on the rugged North coast of Cornwall, you will find Port Isaac, a captivating fishing village steeped in history that has stood the test of time. From its roots as a thriving port during the tin and lead mining era to featuring in popular TV shows, Port Isaac is a quintessential coastal village that enchants both locals and tourists alike.

Its rich history dates back to the 14th century under the name "Port Izzat," which served as a bustling trade port for Cornwall's tin mining industry until the 19th century. Iconic buildings such as the harbor walls and old fish cellars were constructed from nearby Delabole limestone quarry. Port Isaac's winding streets and alleyways have housed many notable figures throughout history, including the writer Thomas Hardy and artist John Opie.

St. Peter's Church, a 14th-century landmark, is perched atop a cliff overlooking the harbor, making for a breathtaking view. It also has a significant role in many films and TV shows, including the hit series "Doc Martin." The harbor area boasts colorful cottages and vibrant fishing boats, and the Port Isaac Heritage Center educates visitors on the village's fishing heritage.

Port Isaac harbors a strong sense of community with unique traditions, such as the Fisherman's Friends' Christmas procession, where carolers wander through the streets singing traditional carols. You can find quaint local businesses in the village, including art galleries, shops selling locally-made crafts, and charming bed and breakfasts that promise a comfortable stay.

The unique landscape is another standout feature of Port Isaac, with its rugged coastline and rolling hills that add to its charm. The village is located in an Area of Outstanding Natural Beauty, and visitors can embark on breathtaking coastal walks on the South West Coast Path. Those interested in history can visit the legendary birthplace of King Arthur at the nearby Tintagel Castle.

While Port Isaac has remained true to its heritage, it has also evolved with time. The Michelin-starred restaurant, Nathan Outlaw, is a new development that has expanded its culinary options. Port Isaac has also gained global fame as the filming location for the popular TV show "Doc Martin," attracting fans worldwide to see the locations. Yet, its unique character and sense of community remain unchanged, continuing to captivate residents and visitors alike.

Bourton-on-the-Water

Nestled amidst the Cotswold Hills of Gloucestershire lays a quaint and charming village that has captured the imaginations of travelers from all over the world. Bourton-on-the-Water is a hidden gem that boasts unique waterways and picturesque bridges that stand the test of time. Visiting the village is like stepping back in time, only to be surrounded by modern-day attractions that are sure to amaze.

The village traces back to the Roman era as a bustling settlement. Bourton-on-the-Water's name came from the Saxon word "bourne," meaning "stream," which is fitting since the village is famous for its intriguing series of shallow streams that flow through its center. The region's Middle Ages were critical in the development of the village's key industries, cloth, and paper, which were once powered by the steady flow of the mill.

An iconic feature of the village is the elegant arched bridge that spans the River Windrush. The bridge, built-in 1654, is world-famous and known as the "Venice of the Cotswolds." The model village, a one-ninth scale replica of the village itself, is another must-see attraction, bringing visitors in search of the town's beauty's delightful waterways and famous buildings like the Church of St. Lawrence and Victoria Hall.

The village has friendly streets that are lined with charming shops and delightful local eateries, making it the perfect place to while away a lazy afternoon.

The village is a buzzing community, with different events throughout the year. From the Cotswold Show in July to the lighting ceremony of the Christmas tree in December, there are endless activities for visitors to enjoy. The Cotswold Perfumery is another unique attraction — a must-visit offering bespoke fragrances, and visitors can even create their personalized scent.

Bourton-on-the-Water's natural surroundings are stunning, with the Cotswold Hills serving a beautiful backdrop. The hills provide plenty of opportunities for outdoor activities such as hiking and cycling. The nearby nature reserve at Greystones Farm also provides visitors with the chance to do some birdwatching and observe the local fauna.

Despite its popularity with tourists, Bourton-on-the-Water has retained its charm, and the village has a strong community spirit. The village has several amenities, a primary school, a post office, medical center — making it the perfect spot for families.

Haworth

Discovering the Literary and Cultural Landmark of Haworth Village
Nestled in the stunning West Yorkshire landscape, Haworth is a small village with a rich history and breathtaking scenery that continues to attract visitors from far and wide. However, it's the village's connection to the Brontë sisters that sets it apart as a literary and cultural landmark of the 19th century.

History buffs and literature enthusiasts alike must visit the Haworth Parsonage, the historic home where the Brontë family lived for over 40 years and where the sisters wrote some of their most famous works. Today, the parsonage is a museum that showcases the family's life and work.

Haworth also boasts a wealth of landmarks and cultural sites that pay tribute to the Brontës' legacy. Take a hike along the moors to discover the Brontë Waterfall, a picturesque natural monument that famously inspired Emily Brontë's masterpiece, Wuthering Heights. The St. Michael and All Angels' Church is another significant landmark and a spiritual cornerstone of the community.

As you explore the charming cobbled streets, you'll discover cozy cafes and independent shops that add to the village's unique character. Locals love Cobbles & Clay, serving homemade cakes and hot cups of tea in a warm, inviting atmosphere. The Haworth Old School Room regularly hosts art exhibitions and workshops that showcase the village's creative side.

If you time your visit just right, you might be lucky enough to experience one of Haworth's cherished local traditions. The annual Haworth Fair takes place every November and attracts visitors from all over. Literary events like the Brontë Festival of Women's Writing and the Haworth Arts Festival celebrate the sisters' enduring impact on literature and culture.

But perhaps the most enduring aspect of village life in Haworth is its stunning natural landscape. The rolling hills and winding moors offer a timeless escape from the hustle and bustle of modern life. The Brontës' deep appreciation for nature is evident in their writings, and taking a walk along the moors is a chance to see firsthand the beauty that inspired some of their most haunting and supernatural scenes.

Whether you're a fan of literature, history, or just seeking a unique travel experience, Haworth is sure to capture your heart with its timeless charm. From the enduring legacy of the Brontë sisters to the warmth and welcoming spirit of its community, this West Yorkshire gem is a must-see for anyone seeking to explore the beauty and history of the UK's villages.

Mousehole

The charming village of Mousehole can be found nestled on the picturesque coast of Cornwall in the southwest of England. With a deep and fascinating history that spans centuries, Mousehole is a cultural hotspot that attracts visitors from every corner of the globe. Famous for its rich fishing heritage, the village was once a bustling port where local fishermen braved the waves to bring in their catch, with a particular reputation for pilchard fishing.

Despite its quaint appearance, Mousehole boasts several landmarks that are steeped in history, such as St Clement's Island, which is accessible on foot at low tide and offers breathtaking views of the coast. In addition to these cultural sites, Mousehole also has a proud local community with a strong sense of community spirit, which is evident in the various events that take place throughout the year. These include the famous Christmas lights display that draws in visitors from far and wide, which began in the 1960s when artist Joan Gillchrest decided to bring a little magic to the village during the long winter nights. Mousehole also plays host to a traditional Cornish festival, complete with folk music, dancing, and local food.

The town is filled with unique local businesses, including a traditional bakery and artisanal shops selling one-of-a-kind souvenirs. The area surrounding the village is a naturally stunning landscape, complete with sandy beaches, rugged cliffs, and crystal-clear waters. There are also several coastal walks, including the South West Coast Path, which offer breathtaking views of the stunning coastline. Mousehole is living history, a place where unique traditions and rich culture create an inviting atmosphere filled with warmth and community. A visit to this hidden treasure is an experience not to be missed.

In addition to its rich cultural heritage, Mousehole is also a hub for creative arts. The village has inspired many artists and writers over the years, with its stunning scenery and unique character. It is home to several galleries and studios where local artists showcase their work, including paintings, sculpture, and pottery. The Mousehole Arts Festival, held annually in the summer, is a celebration of the village's artistic community, featuring live music, workshops, and exhibitions. The festival is a testament to the village's creative spirit, which continues to thrive to this day. Whether you're a history buff, an art lover, or simply looking for a charming coastal getaway, Mousehole is the perfect destination. Its warm and welcoming atmosphere, combined with its stunning natural beauty and rich cultural heritage, make it a truly special place to visit.

Rye

There's something undeniably special about Rye, a picturesque little village nestled in the heart of southern England. Its rich history stretches back to medieval times, and to this day, it preserves the medieval charm that draws visitors from across the globe. Among the few towns in the UK that have managed to hold onto their historic character, this old seaport has a unique charisma all its own.

Rye's place in English history is long and storied. It was founded in the 12th century and served as a seaport for centuries afterward. During the medieval period, it was an essential hub for trading ships that sailed along the English Channel. And the town's streets have hosted their fair share of prominent figures, from merchants to explorers and everything in between.

Walking through Rye's ancient streets, it's hard not to feel transported back in time. Cobbled roads and winding alleyways hark back to its past as a fortified port town. There are secret nooks and crannies around every corner, ready for exploration. And even the town's gates, the Ypres Tower and Landgate, have been standing tall for close to eight hundred years.

But Rye isn't just a well-preserved relic from the past. Its vibrant community keeps it thriving in the present day. With independent tea shops, bakeries, and restaurants alongside bustling community activities, there's never a shortage of things to do. And the village's literary and artistic heritage is an integral part of its identity, celebrated in various festivals throughout the year.

Rye's beauty isn't limited just to the town itself, either. Venture out to nearby Winchelsea Beach, and you'll be treated to stunning views of the English Channel. And despite its status as a historical relic, Rye isn't stuck in the past. Its modern developments and friendly atmosphere make it a perfect place for visitors to stay or even choose for their home base.

All in all, Rye's combination of medieval charm, rich history, and friendly community spirit make it a must-see destination for anyone interested in the United Kingdom and its countless treasures.

Shanklin

Nestled on the southern coast of the enchanting Isle of Wight, you will find the quaint and picturesque village of Shanklin. The village has managed to preserve its old-world charm amid the hustle and bustle of modern life. Shanklin has a unique history, natural surroundings, landmarks, traditions, and current aspects of village life that make it stand out as a vital addition to any tour of the UK.

Shanklin's history goes back to the early medieval period when the village was popular for pastoral agriculture and fishing. Even notable historical figures such as Queen Victoria visited the charming village in the mid-1800s. In World War II, Shanklin suffered from bombings, but the village has risen and will continue to thrive.

One of the most popular landmarks in Shanklin is the natural wonder that is the Shanklin Chine. Visitors can wander along the paths, taking in the lush vegetation, cascading waterfalls, and stunning views. Shanklin Theatre is another landmark that attracts those with an interest in the arts.

The Old Village is a cultural site, adorned with unique architecture and thatched cottages, providing a sense of nostalgia for those interested in the history of the area. The community spirit is alive and well in Shanklin as it plays host to numerous events like the Old Gaffers Festival, a delightful nautical event celebrating boats from days gone by. Visitors can also engage in community activities such as carol services and tree lighting events during Christmas.

Shanklin's natural surroundings and landscape, particularly the pristine sand of the beaches and shores, make for an excellent spot for water sports enthusiasts. You can hike to the top of the downs to get a breathtaking view of the village and the beautiful surrounding countryside.

Today, Shanklin is a thriving hub of tourism, making it easy for visitors to explore and enjoy the beauty of the Isle of Wight in comfort. The community spirit in Shanklin is strong, and there is a thriving local economy, making it an ideal village to call home.

In conclusion, Shanklin's old village charm and thatched cottages, combined with its stunning natural wonders and cultural events, make it a must-visit destination on any tour of the UK. The village is a hidden gem that should not be missed.

Bugbrooke

As you step into Bugbrooke, a quaint village nestled in the heart of Northamptonshire, you'll find yourself transported to a different time and place. Here, amidst its picturesque landscapes, you'll discover a rich history, unique traditions, and a close-knit community that has stood the test of time.

At the center of Bugbrooke stands Heygate Mill, a heritage site that has been a staple of the village for centuries. From its humble beginnings as a traditional flour mill in the 19th century to its modern-day incarnation as a sophisticated milling operation, Heygate Mill has played a critical role in shaping the village's fortunes. The Heygate family, who have been milling flour in Bugbrooke since the 16th century, have been the driving force behind this evolution and have been instrumental in the growth and development of the village for generations.

But Bugbrooke isn't just about its rich past. The village played a vital role in the English Civil War and was a refuge for soldiers on both sides during the Battle of Naseby. It is also believed that the famous philosopher John Locke stayed in the village during his time as a tutor at Christ Church College.

As you explore Bugbrooke, you'll discover that there's much more to it than its heritage sites. The local pet store is the heart and soul of the community and a charming meeting place where locals come to connect and catch up. The village's festivals, including St. Michael's Day and the "Wife Selling" fair, are a testament to Bugbrooke's vibrant culture and its residents' community spirit.

The village's natural beauty is equally captivating. The grandeur of the rolling hills that surround Bugbrooke, the stunning vistas of the farmlands, and the tranquil waterways such as the Grand Union Canal are perfect for a leisurely stroll or bike ride. With so much to see, explore, and enjoy in and around Bugbrooke, it's no wonder the village is a popular destination for tourists and locals alike.

If you're looking to escape the hustle and bustle of city life and want to experience the essence of England in all its glory, Bugbrooke should be on your list. It is a true gem that encapsulates the charm, history, and community spirit that define this country.

Hambleden

Discovering Hambleden: A Hidden Gem of Rural England
Nestled in the breathtaking Chiltern Hills of Buckinghamshire lies Hambleden, an idyllic English village that truly embodies the charm of countryside living. With a population of approximately four hundred, this tight-knit community boasts its deep roots and stunning natural environment. What sets Hambleden apart is its ability to attract filmmakers, thanks to its timeless architecture and unspoiled vistas that have been featured in a variety of popular TV shows and movies like 'Chitty Chitty Bang Bang' and 'Midsomer Murders.'

Hambleden's rich history dates back to the 1086 Domesday Book, and the village is steeped in heritage and culture. In medieval times, it was a thriving market town, and the remnants of a 14th-century market cross are still visible today. The church of St. Mary the Virgin is equally awe-inspiring, with its impressive Gothic Revival tower that was built in the 12th century. It's thought to be one of the oldest surviving churches in the region, boasting a stunning 16th-century brass chandelier, one of only a handful left in England. The 17th-century Hambleden Mill has also been converted into a luxurious place to stay.

Hambleden's picturesque atmosphere has made it a sought-after location for shooting various films and TV series, including 'The Witches,' 'A Christmas Carol,' 'Miss Marple: The Mirror Crack'd from Side to Side,' 'Midsomer Murders,' 'Lewis,' and 'Endeavour.' Exploring the filming locations around the village adds an exciting element to any visit.

Nature lovers will be left in awe by Hambleden's stunning countryside. The village is situated in the vast Area of Outstanding Natural Beauty that is the Chiltern Hills, with walking trails and breathtaking views that will leave you inspired. The nearby Hambleden Valley features the River Thames winding through, providing a haven for bird species and other wildlife that call the valley home.

The true heart of Hambleden lies in its warm community and local businesses. The village hosts a range of vibrant events every year, such as the annual fair and Guy Fawkes Night firework display. The area also has a few noteworthy local businesses, including the lively Hare and Hounds pub, the quaint Apple Orchard farm shop, and the small independent brewery Rebellion Beer.

Plan your trip to Hambleden to experience the essence of traditional English village life combined with magnificent nature walks and a welcoming community. History fans, movie buffs, nature enthusiasts, and those who enjoy supporting local businesses will find plenty to love in this hidden gem of rural England.

Kersey

If you're looking for a charming village that showcases England's rich heritage, then look no further than Kersey. Part of the "100 Random Villages in the UK," Kersey is nestled in the heart of Suffolk and boasts medieval streets and a storied history that will transport you back in time.

Step back into the Middle Ages, when Kersey was a bustling marketplace for wool and cloth, known for its expert tradespeople and artisanal skills. All Saints Church, built in the 14th century with funds donated by wealthy cloth merchant John de Wolverstone, still stands today and serves as a testament to the village's rich history.

In the 16th century, Kersey became a center for Puritanism and continues to reflect this religious influence in several historic buildings throughout the village. Today, Kersey is home to many cultural sites and landmarks, including the iconic All Saints Church and Kersey Pottery, which has been producing handmade pottery for over 60 years.

One of the village's unique traditions is the Kersey Open Gardens event, where residents open their gardens to the public and display their impressive horticultural skills. Visitors can explore the village on guided walks, visit the country market stalls, and enjoy a break in one of the many tea rooms.

The River Brett flows through the heart of Kersey, offering a picturesque setting for fishing, picnics, and river walks. The village's community spirit is visible in the many events and activities organized throughout the year, including the Kersey Festival, held every other year, which fills the streets with music, dancing, and family-friendly activities.

When you visit Kersey, be sure to stop by The Bell Inn, a bustling hub for residents and visitors to sample local beer and hearty British fare. With its medieval streets and historic significance, Kersey exudes charm, intrigue, and a warm community spirit that makes it a must-visit destination for any traveler.

Lavenham

Nestled in the heart of Suffolk lies Lavenham, a sleepy, picturesque village filled with rich history and traditions, preserved for centuries. As one of the most well-preserved medieval wool trading centers in the UK, Lavenham is a must-see destination for anyone interested in cultural and historical heritage.

Lavenham was once a bustling market village that grew wealthy from wool trading in the 14th and 15th centuries. It was one of the wealthiest wool towns in the country, attracting merchants from all over England and beyond. Some notable historical figures who shaped the village's wool trade include John Wymond, who built the imposing De Vere House, and William De Lavenham, who gave his name to the village.

As the wool trade declined during the 16th century, Lavenham became a "sleepy" village that remained unchanged for decades. However, in the late 19th and early 20th century, Lavenham experienced a renaissance with the arrival of tourists drawn by its medieval charm.

Visitors will revel in Lavenham's key landmarks, including the Guildhall and the Little Hall, a medieval house turned museum. The Guildhall was built in the 16th century and served as a meeting place for the wool merchants. It's now a museum showcasing the village's wool trade and customs.

De Vere House, an iconic timber-framed house in the center of the village, is a popular destination for Harry Potter fans. It's believed to have inspired J.K. Rowling's depiction of fictional character Godric's Hollow.

Lavenham prides itself on its community spirit, reflected in the annual events that unite locals and visitors alike. The Lavenham Christmas Fair, held every December, is a festive event featuring local crafts, food, and entertainment. The Lavenham Literary Festival, held in November, brings together authors, book lovers, and literary enthusiasts from all over the world.

Lavenham's unique establishments display the village's character and charm. The Swan Hotel, a Grade-II listed building, offers visitors a glimpse into the village's medieval past, with its wooden beams and open fires. The Lavenham Butcher is a traditional, family-run business selling locally sourced meat and other specialty products. The village's art galleries and craft shops offer a wide variety of handmade products, including pottery, jewelry, and textiles.

Lavenham is surrounded by breathtaking natural scenery, including the Dedham Vale Area of Outstanding Natural Beauty and the Stour Valley, making it an ideal base for exploring the lush landscapes and peaceful trails that weave through the area.

Beddgelert

As you journey through the breathtaking Snowdonia mountains, you'll stumble upon a hidden gem, an enchanting village known as Beddgelert. With a name that translates to Gelert's Grave, Beddgelert is a place that overflows with historical legends, natural wonders, and charming traditions.

As the legend goes, Prince Llywelyn the Great's faithful hunting dog, Gelert, was unjustly slain by his grieving master. The village pays tribute to the legend with Gelert's Grave, a place where visitors can reflect upon the tragic tale. Beddgelert was also a significant slate mining hub in the 19th century, and visitors can traverse the former mining site, Sygun Copper Mine, which now serves as a popular tourist destination.

The picturesque village has several notable landmarks, including St. Mary's Church. The church is a remarkable structure that dates back to the 14th century and features a stained-glass window that tells the story of the famed legend. Furthermore, the Aberglaslyn Pass, part of the Snowdonia National Park, is a historic and picturesque gorge that serves as a favorite spot for fishing, hiking, and birdwatching.

In addition to being a tight-knit community, the village boasts a thriving arts scene with galleries, cafes, and markets showcasing the area's handmade products and crafts. Visitors can also indulge themselves in local deliciousness from renowned businesses such as Glaslyn Ices, which serves up award-winning homemade ice cream with locally sourced ingredients.

The village's natural beauty is a significant attraction that never ceases to amaze. With the Snowdon mountain overlooking it, Beddgelert is a great spot to indulge in outdoor activities, including white-water rafting and kayaking while enjoying the mesmerizing landscape features like waterfalls and the Glaslyn Estuary.

Even though the mining industry has long disappeared, tourism remains the driving force of the village's economy. The locals remain ever welcoming to visitors and are proud to share their knowledge of the area and its cultural significance.

In conclusion, Beddgelert is a charming village that packs in an impressive blend of natural beauty, historical significance, and cultural traditions. Whether you're seeking adventure, relaxation, or cultural enrichment, you're sure to be captivated by the unique appeal of the village and the memories it holds.

Plockton

The serene village of Plockton, nestled on the west coast of Scotland, has been captivating people for centuries. Its stunning views and thriving community have made it a beloved destination for visitors and locals alike.

In the 19th century, Plockton served as a bustling fishing port, supplying herring to the country and beyond. Its strategic location also made it a frequent stop for the Royal Navy during World War II. Today, it's best known for its literary history, thanks to Gavin Maxwell's book "Ring of Bright Water" and his vivid descriptions of village life and surroundings.

Another highlight of Plockton is the iconic Duncraig Castle, built in the mid-19th century and with a fascinating history. The castle has served as a hospital during World War II and as a location for movies over the years. It now hosts a range of special events and occasions.

The Gaelic college - Sabhal Mòr Ostaig - is also a must-see for visitors, with its role in promoting Gaelic language and culture. The campus boasts some of the most breathtaking views of the landscape, including the iconic Cuillin Hills.

Plockton's natural surroundings are one of its biggest attractions, including the stunning Loch Carron stretching out to one side and hills rising up in the distance. The mild climate allows for unique plant species to flourish in the area, adding to the village's charm.

Plockton's traditional music scene is also highly celebrated, with several local bands and frequent music festivals. The village is also home to several independent businesses, including the famous Plockton Inn, which offers patrons a chance to dine on traditional Scottish dishes while taking in the picturesque harbor views.

As its charm and beauty continue to draw visitors from around the world, it's no surprise that Plockton has become a beloved spot for anyone looking to connect with Scotland's rich history and culture. A trip to this picturesque village is a chance to experience the unique spirit of community and natural wonder that the village embodies.

Bamburgh

Located on the Northumberland coast, just a stone's throw away from the Scottish border, Bamburgh is a quaint and charming village that paints a captivating picture of the past. Its history dates back to over 1,400 years, with the first settlement dating back to the 6th century. It was once a site of great significance for the Anglo-Saxon kings of Northumbria and was later seized by Vikings in the 10th century. Saint Aidan, who was an Irish-born monk, founded a monastery in the area in the 7th century, turning it into a pilgrimage site during the Middle Ages.

However, Bamburgh's most iconic attraction is undoubtedly the stunning Bamburgh Castle. Founded in the 11th century by the Normans, it is an awe-inspiring site to behold and a must-visit spot for history lovers. It has undergone several renovations over the years and currently houses a collection of ancient artefacts and furniture, including the elaborate armour of past inhabitants. Its winding staircases, subterranean passages, and hidden rooms all add to its mysterious charm.

Aside from the castle, visitors can also explore other historical landmarks in the village. One such attraction is the Grace Darling Museum, named after a local heroine who became famous after she rescued shipwrecked sailors. The museum boasts original exhibits about her life, as well as other displays that focus on the region's seafaring history.

Tourists who love nature will also delight in the village's natural surroundings. Visitors can take a stroll along miles of golden sandy beaches, with stunning views of the picturesque Farne Islands, where puffins and grey seals reside. These coastal areas are excellent for soaking in the village's unique character and charm.

The Bamburgh Ploughing Festival, held annually, is an agricultural festival that showcases the village's strong sense of community spirit and unique traditions. The festival features various competitions, including tractor driving and horse-drawn plowing, and attracts visitors from all over the county.

In recent years, Bamburgh has emerged as a culinary destination, with numerous boutique cafes, excellent restaurants, and specialty shops run by talented local vendors that serve the best of the region's food and drink produce. Its warm and welcoming community with a strong sense of community spirit makes it a special place to visit or call home. Bamburgh is a quintessential seaside village engulfed in an aura of delightful warmth, enriched with history, and boasting a stunning coastal beauty that will leave visitors breathless.

Robin Hood's Bay

Nestled on the windswept North Yorkshire coastline lies the picturesque village of Robin Hood's Bay. This charming corner of the UK is steeped in history and natural beauty, and has been capturing the hearts of travelers for centuries. Robin Hood's Bay has a rich history, with a particularly fascinating past as a bustling port and center for smuggling activities. In the 18th century, the village was known as the "Smugglers' Den," and was home to notorious smugglers such as Joseph 'King' Bell and Frankie and Johnny Dawson. Despite the decline of its fortunes in the 19th century due to the rise of larger ports along the coast, the village retains its unique charm and character.

Visitors to Robin Hood's Bay have much to explore, with several historical and cultural landmarks. The Old Coastguard Station is a notable site, functioning as a museum where visitors can learn about the area's seafaring and smuggling past, as well as discover displays of local flora and fauna. St Stephen's Church is also a must-visit, with its stunning stained glass windows and peaceful atmosphere. For the adventurous and curious, the village's narrow streets and staircases, such as the famous "Ginnel" which leads down to the seafront, provide plenty of exploration.

Robin Hood's Bay's rugged coastline is one of its most breathtaking geographic features, with the village perched on a steep hillside offering stunning views of the sea. Visitors can explore the bay itself, home to secluded coves, rock pools, and hidden caves. The village is situated near some of the most scenic natural areas in the UK, including the North York Moors and the Yorkshire Dales.

In Robin Hood's Bay, visitors will find a vibrant community of locals and visitors alike. The village hosts an annual Folk Weekend, featuring musicians from around the region, as well as other local events including a Christmas fair and a summer festival. Visitors can indulge in the village's famous fish and chips, or browse its quirky independent shops and galleries.

Today, Robin Hood's Bay continues to captivate travelers from around the world, drawing them with its rich history and natural beauty. The village has a strong sense of community, with locals coming together for events and activities. For anyone interested in history, culture, and adventure, this picturesque corner of the UK is a must-visit.

Bossington

Nestled along the picturesque shores of the Bristol Channel, Bossington Village is a tranquil haven with a distinct charm that is hard to miss. As one of the 100 Random Villages in the UK, Bossington is renowned for its natural allure and wildlife, which attract visitors from far and wide.

Bossington Village boasts a rich history that traces back to the 13th century. It was under the ownership of the affluent Tynte family, but it wasn't until the 16th century that the village gained prominence. At this time, it became notorious for smuggling activities, attracting wealthy characters like Captain Kidd and Jack Rattenbury.

A prominent attraction in Bossington is the All Saints Church. The church, believed to date back to the 12th century, was restored in the 15th century and features a striking west tower dating from the early 16th century.

Another remarkable landmark in the town is the National Trust Selworthy Green, which features delightful open space surrounded by thatched cottages and is a top cultural site in Bossington.

One of the most popular events in Bossington is the annual traditional Christmas Carol Concert, an event that brings together both villagers and visitors to celebrate the holiday season inside the beautiful All Saints Church amidst local music performances.

Bossington's surrounding natural beauty is one of its most sought-after features. The village is located in the midst of Exmoor National Park, boasting breathtaking rolling hills and steep coastal cliffs. Visitors can take a leisurely stroll along the Bossington beach, hike up to the top of the cliffs or explore the picturesque countryside that surrounds the village while enjoying the abundant wildlife, such as wild ponies and red deer.

Bossington is home to a plethora of local spots offering unique experiences to both visitors and locals. From quaint teahouses, local pubs to various shops selling handmade gifts and souvenirs, the village has something on offer for everyone. Additionally, the village boasts a vibrant community spirit that's evident throughout the year, with events such as the Bossington Open Gardens Day and the Bossington Summer Fair.

Overall, Bossington is a quintessential English village ideal anyone vying for a peaceful escape from the urban frenzy. With its stunning natural beauty, rich history, cultural sites, vivid village life, and abundant wildlife, Bossington should be at the top of your travel list. It's a destination that will leave you with unforgettable memories.

Grasmere

Explore the Hidden Literary Treasure of the Lake District National Park: Grasmere

Grasmere, a quaint village nestled in the heart of the Lake District National Park, is bursting with character and history. Despite its larger and more well-known neighboring towns, Windermere and Ambleside, Grasmere stands out with its unique charm that captivates locals and tourists alike.

Grasmere's rich history dates back to the Viking era, and during the medieval period, it became a hub for monasteries. The wool trade brought prosperity to the village, but it was during the 18th and 19th centuries that Grasmere became a literary center. The village was home to William Wordsworth, Samuel Taylor Coleridge, and Thomas De Quincey, among others.

William Wordsworth's connection to Grasmere is perhaps the most famous literary feature of the village. Wordsworth lived there for over a decade and found inspiration in the natural surroundings to write some of his most famous works, including the iconic poem "I Wandered Lonely as a Cloud" or "Daffodils." Dove Cottage, where Wordsworth lived with his sister Dorothy, has been turned into a museum that offers visitors a glimpse into Wordsworth's living quarters and his life and work.

Aside from Dove Cottage, other landmarks that attract tourists to Grasmere include St. Oswald's Church, the Wordsworth Memorial and Museum, and the Heaton Cooper Studio. Grasmere's community spirit adds to its old-world charm, offering traditional sports like Cumberland wrestling, fell running, and hound trailing, as well as the annual Grasmere Lakeland Sports and Show.

Grasmere's stunning natural surroundings include Grasmere Lake, which is perfect for boating, and the surrounding hills, including Helm Crag and Silver Howe, which offer stunning walks and views of the village. For the more adventurous, the Fairfield Horseshoe hike around the extensive range of fells surrounding Grasmere is a great option.

Despite modernisation, Grasmere has retained its old-world charm, with quaint cafes, pubs, and specialty shops showcasing locally made products and souvenirs. The village also offers accommodation options for all budgets, including guest houses, bed and breakfasts, and hotels.

In conclusion, Grasmere may be small in size, but it is a destination that caters to all interests with its literary connections, stunning natural surroundings, and thriving community spirit, making it one of the UK's hidden gems.

Tobermory

The lovely and lively village of Tobermory can be found nestled on the Isle of Mull off the rugged west coast of Scotland. Its charming Gaelic name, Tobar Mhoire, roughly translates to "Mary's well," a nod to the sacred spring which once flowed in the area. The village is well-known for its colorful seafront - a row of buildings that paints a stunning sight on the shoreline - and for being home to a thriving marine life.

Once a bustling port where ships came from around Europe and beyond to trade in tobacco, wool, timber, exotic spices, and more, Tobermory was founded in 1788 by the British Fisheries Society for herring fishing and processing. Visitors can marvel at the numerous historical figures associated with the area, such as Lachlan Macquarie, a Scottish soldier and colonial administrator who was born in the nearby island of Ulva and who helped to establish New South Wales, Australia.

Tobermory has more to offer than just a rich history and stunning seafront, of course. The Mull Museum houses local history and culture, while the Tobermory Distillery is a must-visit for whisky aficionados. Visitors can explore the rich marine life in the area as well, with over 250 species of fish and 100 species of seaweed in the waters alongside invertebrates and mammals such as otters, whales, and dolphins. The village is also home to the first marine reserve in Scotland, the Tobermory Marine Reserve, where visitors can partake in snorkeling, diving, and kayaking.

Despite its remote location and small population of less than 1,000 inhabitants, Tobermory has a thriving community scene, with events like the Mull Music Festival, the Mull Highland Games, and the Tobermory Lifeboat Day drawing people from far and wide. The Isle of Mull Cheese Company and An Tobar, a contemporary arts center that hosts performances and workshops, are just some of the local businesses that showcase the island's produce and crafts.

In conclusion, Tobermory is a lively and unique village that has something to offer everyone, whether you're a nature lover, whisky enthusiast, or just seeking a peaceful getaway. Its stunning seafront and thriving marine life are just a few of the many reasons it's worth a visit, and the village is sure to capture your heart with its rich history and lovely community vibe. It comes as no surprise that once you have visited, you may find yourself echoing Charles Lamb's statement: "If there be a paradise on earth, it cannot be far from Tobermory."

Warkworth

Warkworth is a historic and charming village nestled in Northumberland region that draws in history buffs, cultural enthusiasts, and travel aficionados from all over the world. With its rich cultural landmarks, unique traditions, and modern community spirit, Warkworth has something truly special to offer to visitors and residents alike.

The roots of Warkworth date back to the 8th century, with the establishment of a monastery that was later destroyed during Viking raids. However, it was later rebuilt in the 12th century as a fortified castle commissioned by Henry, son of David I of Scotland, who later became the Earl of Northumberland. Over the years, the castle became a key stronghold in various military conflicts, including the Scottish Wars of Independence and the Wars of the Roses. It was also home to several notable figures, including the Percy family, who played an important role in English history and the infamous Harry Hotspur, who was immortalized by Shakespeare in his plays.

At the heart of Warkworth's historical significance is its famous castle, a stunning example of 14th century military architecture in Europe and a must-visit for history enthusiasts. Another key landmark is the nearby church of St. Lawrence, dating back to the 12th century and featuring stunning examples of medieval architecture.

Warkworth is also renowned for its unique traditions and community activities. The village holds an annual Warkworth Show, a traditional agricultural show featuring competitions, displays, and activities since 1852, allowing visitors to experience the charm of rural Northumberland. Local businesses add to the village's charm, from boutique shops to galleries, artisan food producers, and cafes, displaying the creativity and innovation of the local community.

The village's natural surroundings are another key aspect of its appeal since the village is set in the stunning Northumberland countryside, surrounded by rolling hills, verdant farmland, and stunning coastal scenery. Nearby attractions include the Northumberland National Park, the Alnwick Garden, and the Farne Islands.

Today, Warkworth is a vibrant and welcoming village, boasting a strong sense of community and a range of amenities and attractions. From its castle and church to its local businesses and breathtaking countryside, Warkworth has something for everyone. Whether you're a history buff, a lover of culture and tradition, or just looking for a beautiful place to visit or live in, Warkworth has it all.

Betws-y-Coed

Nestled deep in the heart of Snowdonia National Park, lies the charming village of Betws-y-Coed, a gem of North Wales that has captivated the hearts of many avid travelers and outdoor enthusiasts worldwide. Boasting stunning natural scenery, a rich history, and a thriving community, Betws-y-Coed is the perfect destination for anyone seeking adventure, culture, and tranquility.

Dating back to the early 13th century, Betws-y-Coed has a long and fascinating history, attracting visitors from far and wide thanks to its picturesque location and breathtaking surroundings. And it's not just the historical aspects that make it so special; the village is filled with key landmarks and cultural sites that reflect the area's unique traditions and customs. St. Mary's Church, a 14th-century building in the village center, is a must-visit. And the picture-perfect stone structure, Pont-y-Pair Bridge, is another popular attraction that crosses the River Llugwy.

What makes this village truly unique is its community culture, where close-knit and vibrant locals celebrate their traditions with pride and enthusiasm. The annual Betws-y-Coed Carnival is a celebration of their Welsh heritage and folklore, with music, dancing, and street performances that will leave you in awe. Additionally, visitors can take home a piece of Welsh culture by purchasing traditional Welsh crafts at Tŷ Hyll, the famous Welsh craft shop located in the village.

One of the main draws of Betws-y-Coed is undoubtedly the unspoiled natural surroundings that offer peace and tranquility to visitors. The village is the starting point for several of Snowdonia's best-known walks and treks, including the beautiful Swallow Falls Trail, with cascading waterfalls and stunning rock formations. Add to that the sparkling lakes, rushing streams, and breathtaking mountain ranges, and you have yourself a paradise for outdoor enthusiasts. Fishing, cycling, hiking, and other outdoor pursuits are among the activities that await you.

Today, Betws-y-Coed remains a popular destination among travelers who seek to escape the hustle and bustle of daily life and find themselves surrounded by nature, culture, and a welcoming community. Throughout the year, the village hosts several events and festivals, such as the Snowdonia Arts Festival, making it an exciting and vibrant place for visitors of all ages.

In conclusion, Betws-y-Coed is truly one of the UK's most beautiful and unique villages that offer visitors an opportunity to embrace Welsh culture, explore the natural landscape, and connect with the local community. Whether you're a seasoned traveler or a first-time visitor, Betws-y-Coed is a must-see destination that guarantees a lasting impression.

Crail

Nestled in the East Neuk of Fife, Scotland, the picturesque village of Crail is a perennial favorite among visitors looking to experience its historic harbor and thriving fishing industry. The friendly locals, unique culture and scenic beauty of the area make Crail a must-visit destination in the UK.

Crail's rich history stretches all the way back to the 12th century, bearing witness to significant changes over the centuries. The village was known as Kilrenny back then and it soon began to thrive as a trading hub, after being granted the right to hold a market by King David I. By the 16th century, Crail's harbor became a shipbuilding hub, producing the famous "Krames" trading and fishing vessels. At its peak in the 18th century, Crail was one of the largest herring ports in Scotland.

The village is home to historic landmarks and cultural sites, including the 14th-century St. Mary's Parish Church located in the heart of the village, the 17th and 18th century buildings surrounding the Toll Booth marketplace, and the Crail Museum and Heritage Centre, where visitors can learn more about the fishing industry, local history, and cultural traditions.

Crail's harbor remains integral to the village's identity and is still used by local fishermen today. The harbor, along with several seafood restaurants and cafes, is a central feature that visitors can take a leisurely stroll along and watch the boats coming in and out.

Crail's community hosts unique events and festivals throughout the year, including the annual Crail Food Festival, showcasing the best of Scottish cuisine and local produce, and the Crail Festival that offers live music, theatre, and art. Visitors are welcome to join in on community activities such as choir rehearsals.

The village's coastal location offers visitors plenty of opportunities to explore the great outdoors. Visitors can enjoy scenic walks and picnics amid the farmlands or partake in outdoor activities such as hiking, cycling, and golf.

Despite remaining steeped in tradition, Crail has embraced modern developments, including new cafes, artisan shops, and galleries, adding to the village's charm and vibrancy.

In conclusion, a trip to Crail is a chance to delve into its rich history and culture, explore its historic harbor and thriving fishing industry, and be part of its welcoming community. As a day trip or a potential home, Crail is sure to capture the hearts of all who visit.

Dunster

Nestled in the scenic hills and valleys of western England lies the medieval village of Dunster - a hidden gem waiting to be explored. With centuries of history woven into its fabric, Dunster is a unique village that showcases an old-world charm. Its centerpiece is a majestic castle that has housed several notable historical figures, including the Luttrell family, who lived there for over six centuries.

There is much to see and do in this fascinating village, from visiting the spectacular Grade I listed Dunster Castle to exploring its beautifully preserved buildings, including the 17th-century Yarn Market and the historic Packhorse Bridge, one of Dunster's oldest structures. Marvel at the exquisite woodcarvings that adorn the chapel and altar of the St George's Church or admire the intricate stained-glass windows.

Dunster's sense of tradition and heritage come alive through its annual festivals and events, such as Dunster by Candlelight, when the entire village is illuminated by candlelight, and the Dunster Show, which showcases the best of agricultural and horticultural exhibits. Explore Dunster's natural surroundings by taking a leisurely stroll along the River Avill, an exciting adventure to the Dunkery Beacon for panoramic views of the Exmoor National Park, or visit a local farm to experience the rural life and see animals up close.

Despite its rich past, Dunster is a thriving modern-day village, having retained its close-knit community spirit and vibrant social scene catering to diverse ranges of people. Its local business scene is led by unique shops and boutiques, including the Dunster Dairy Ice Cream, May Cottage Crafts, and Dunster Sweet shop, which is a paradise for anyone with a sweet tooth.

Dunster is a village that exudes an exceptional ambiance, making it a must-visit destination for anyone's UK itinerary. For a true cultural experience, explore the medieval history, landmarks, traditions, and natural surroundings, then immerse yourself in the vibrant modern-day life that Dunster enjoys. This charming village is sure to leave a lasting impression on your heart.

Grasmere

Nestled in the heart of Cumbria County is the charming village of Grasmere. Dubbed the "loveliest spot that man hath ever found" by William Wordsworth himself, this quaint village offers breathtaking natural beauty, rich history, and unique traditions that make it a must-visit destination for anyone exploring the UK.

Grasmere's history dates back to the 7th century, with the construction of the church of St. Oswald, which has since been rebuilt and restored many times. The church is a stunning example of English church architecture and is definitely worth a visit.

Perhaps the most notable historical figure associated with Grasmere is William Wordsworth, who lived in the village with his sister Dorothy for over a decade. The duo composed some of their most famous works, including "I Wandered Lonely as a Cloud." Visitors can tour Wordsworth's Dove Cottage and the adjacent Wordsworth Museum, which houses a vast collection of his manuscripts and personal items.

But it's the natural beauty of Grasmere that truly steals the show. The village is nestled amidst the rolling hills and picturesque valleys of the Lake District, with Lake Grasmere as its centerpiece. The lake offers boating and fishing opportunities, while miles of walking trails surrounding it make it the ideal location for a hike.

In addition to natural beauty, Grasmere is home to unique traditions and community activities. The Grasmere Sports Day, held annually since 1852, features athletic competitions and offers a great way to experience local culture. And you won't want to leave without trying some of the famous Grasmere Gingerbread, made from a recipe dating back to 1854.

Take a stroll through the winding lanes and admire the picturesque Lakeland cottages, or use Grasmere as a base for exploring the Lake District's many attractions. The friendly community, rich history, natural beauty, and local traditions make Grasmere a perfect escape from the hustle and bustle of city life. Whether you're seeking a peaceful retreat or an adventurous weekend getaway, Grasmere won't disappoint.

Eardisland

Discovering the Enchanting Village of Eardisland, Herefordshire
Eardisland is a village that exudes charm and character, situated in the picturesque county of Herefordshire. This stunning destination is one of the UK's most historically significant and breathtaking destinations, drawing visitors from all over the world. Surrounded by rolling hills and verdant fields, Eardisland boasts stunning black and white timber-framed houses and a picturesque River Arrow that runs through its heart.

Eardisland has a rich history dating back to the pre-Roman era, making it stand out among other villages. During the Middle Ages, it was a thriving market town, with many landmarks reflecting this era. One of these landmarks is St. Mary's Church, a 13th-century structure with well-preserved Norman architecture, symbolizing the village's rich heritage.

Today, Eardisland remains a favorite destination for tourists seeking a glimpse of traditional village life in an enchanting historic setting. The village's stunning architecture, including its signature black and white timber-framed buildings, is well-preserved.

The River Arrow, which flows along the village's edge, is another fascinating attraction. It adds to the town's tranquil atmosphere, offering a serene environment perfect for walks and picnics.

Eardisland's welcoming community is notable, and this trait has helped the village maintain its uniqueness and strong sense of identity. The village is also home to a thriving arts community, with many local artists and craftspeople showcasing their work during annual art shows and exhibitions.

May Day is a significant annual celebration in Eardisland, where the community comes together to celebrate the arrival of spring with traditional Morris dancing, music, and other festivities. This celebration is one of the most magnificent traditions in the UK and is well worth a visit.

Eardisland's natural surroundings offer endless possibilities to visitors, with lush green fields surrounding the village on all sides and the River Arrow providing a perfect environment for strolls, picnics, angling, and canoeing. The village's charming pubs, including The Cross Inn, The New Inn, and The White Swan, offer warm and friendly hospitality, providing a perfect base to explore Herefordshire's surrounding areas.

In conclusion, Eardisland is more than just a village; it is an enchanting destination that fully immerses visitors in a traditional English village lifestyle.

Aberdour

Nestled in the enchanting coastal town of Fife, Aberdour is a gem that boasts a blend of rich history and stunning natural beauty. It's a destination that captivates the hearts of visitors with its historical significance, picturesque landmarks, and unique traditions.

Aberdour Castle is the oldest standing castle in the Scottish region, dating back to the twelfth century It's witnessed many significant events throughout its existence and has accommodated influential figures like William Wallace and Mary Queen of Scots. Today, it remains an important historical landmark for Aberdour, with guided tours and exhibitions for visitors.

The village displays exquisite Georgian and Victorian architecture, as seen in the historic St Fillan's Church and Aberdour Hotel. These edifices showcase Aberdour's medieval past and offer characterful accommodations for an authentic Scottish experience. The decorative Cross House and Aberdour Doocot are additional landmarks suitable for exploring.

Aberdour is known for its unique traditions, including the Aberdour Festival, the village's most significant event. This festival brings together locals and visitors in a celebration of community spirit and fun, with music, storytelling, and activities for all ages.

The village's natural surroundings are equally mesmerizing, with stunning beaches like the Black Sands Beach. Walking the Fife Coastal Path enables visitors to discover hidden caves, coves, and magnificent viewpoints to take in.

Today, Aberdour is a thriving community, where local businesses, artisan craft shops, and cafes draw in visitors from all around. From savoring freshly prepared seafood dishes and locally crafted beers to enjoying nature walks, Aberdour provides something for everyone.

In conclusion, Aberdour is a perfect blend of historical significance, coastal charm, and unique traditions that make it one of Scotland's most sought-after destinations. Its rich history and attractive natural landscape offer an exceptional travel experience that creates unforgettable memories for all who visit.

Cartmel

In the verdant hills of Cumbria lies Cartmel, a quaint village steeped in history dating back to medieval times. Visitors are invited to delve into its religious past, indulge in scrumptious puddings, and experience the real charm of rural life in northern England.

Standing tall and proud is the awe-inspiring Augustinian priory, the village's most prominent feature. With intricate carvings and impressive architecture, the priory's imposing tower pierces the skyline and provides a stunning background for photographs. It served as a place of worship for over 800 years, and visitors can take a guided tour to uncover its historical significance.

Cartmel's culinary claim to fame is its sticky toffee pudding, a devilishly divine dessert that has become a must-try for foodies. Comprising a dense, moist cake drenched in creamy toffee sauce, it originated from the village's famous pudding company in the 1970s and has since become a staple across the UK.

The charming village square, lined with historic buildings and home to quaint tearooms, traditional pubs, and artisan shops, is the heart of the community. The tiny racecourse on the outskirts of the village provides a unique countryside experience.

Cartmel hosts community events that bring the village together, such as the annual Cartmel Show, featuring traditional farming displays, local produce, and equestrian events. Farmer's markets are also held regularly, tempting visitors to sample the delicious local produce.

Cartmel's natural surroundings are a tribute to its rural charm and appeal. Tucked away in the Lake District National Park, visitors can feast their eyes on breathtaking landscapes, lakes, and mountain hikes. The Morecambe Bay Area of Outstanding Natural Beauty is also worth exploring.

Despite its rural location, the village brims with community spirit, evident in the friendly and welcoming locals. The tranquil lifestyle and excellent schools have drawn young families to the area in recent years. The village hosts an arts festival that draws visitors from all over the UK and is home to a thriving arts community.

Cartmel is an idyllic destination with a blend of history, tradition, and natural beauty. Its medieval priory, sticky toffee pudding, quaint village square, and outstanding natural beauty make it a unique and memorable experience for all visitors.

Chilham

Nestled in the postcard-perfect county of Kent, Chilham exudes an undeniable charm that will capture your heart. As one of the 100 Random Villages in the UK, this village is a must-visit destination for anyone seeking a dose of traditional English beauty.

Its roots run deep, all the way back to Roman times. Medieval iron production propelled this village into the spotlight, but it's the Digges family's influence during Tudor and Jacobean eras that lead to its flourishing. Notable figures, including none other than Jane Austen herself, have been drawn to the village's intriguing history and charming character.

Chilham's architecture is a seamless fusion of the past and present, with Tudor and Jacobean buildings, such as the imposing Chilham Castle, showcasing the village's rich heritage. Each of these landmarks provides an excellent example of traditional English aesthetics, offering a glimpse into the village's history.

Chilham Square, the centrepiece of the village, remains an integral part of the village's history and tradition. Its surrounding traditional buildings ooze with character and host an array of quaint stores that are perfect for an afternoon of leisurely shopping. Grab a coffee from a local cafe and breathe in the village's warm ambiance.

History and tradition run deep in Chilham. The Harvest and Summer Fairs, cultural and community events in the village, offer a glimpse into the village's vibrant spirit, showcasing a deep sense of warm hospitality and community spirit.

As a village nestled within the Kentish countryside, Chilham's breathtaking natural surroundings are of significant note. A peaceful stroll along the River Stour or a hike in the rolling hills of Kent is sure to rejuvenate and revitalize you. And for those eager for more outdoor adventures, Godmersham Park will not disappoint; a National Trust property, this park is a mecca for outdoor enthusiasts.

As modern developments merge with the village's rich heritage, Chilham is a special place that residents take great pride in calling home. Local businesses, including pubs and village stores, add a unique character to the village.

In conclusion, Chilham is sure to captivate any visitor with its historical heritage, traditional English charm, and lush countryside. Whether you're a history buff, an outdoor enthusiast, or looking to soak in its warm community spirit, this village is a must-visit.

Corfe Castle

Nestled amidst the picturesque beauty of Dorset, Corfe Castle is a treasure trove of historical significance and endless fascination. A small village oozing with mystery and magic, Corfe Castle has been captivating visitors for generations. A storyteller's paradise, each corner of this village is steeped in ancient tales of triumph and tragedy that have left a lasting impact on the region.

A humble castle first built over a millennium ago by William the Conqueror still stands, bearing testament to a glorious history that saw it used as a royal residence for an astounding 500 years. It was even the birthplace of King Edward the Martyr, one of England's celebrated saints. With such rich royal ties, it is not surprising that Corfe Castle has played a pivotal role in the political and military decisions of the country, including critical battles that shaped the nation's future.

The most visible landmark standing today is the castle's keep dominating the town, infusing it with an air of grandeur and magnificence. Visitors can explore the castle ruins, climb its towers and catch breathtaking views of the surrounding village and stunning countryside. With a Grade I listing, St. Edward the Martyr Church is another architectural marvel that one cannot miss. It is a Norman structure, one of the most pristine examples of the style in England. The Corfe Castle Museum and Model Village are both fascinating sites worth exploring.

Corfe Castle wears a friendly and welcoming demeanor, with its close-knit community spreading joy through a variety of activities and traditions. Be it the annual Corfe Castle Carnival or the Food and Drink Festival in autumn, there is always something happening to bring people together. The local businesses add yet another layer to intrigue through their artisanal creations and exquisite offerings. One can indulge in delicious meals, baked goods, and handmade gifts that showcase the best of the region.

Nestled in the Purbeck Hills, the village is a dream come true for nature enthusiasts with endless walking and cycling trails that offer glimpses of glistening beaches, rolling hills, and lush forests. As time flies by, Corfe Castle remains a captivating destination, a testament to its indomitable spirit. Visitors come from all over the world to bask in its rich history, explore its majestic beauty and bask in its vibrant culture. Whether you seek peace, adventure, or a slice of history, Corfe Castle is the perfect destination for you.

Cullen

Step back in time and discover the picturesque village of Cullen, located on the coast of Morayshire, Scotland. Rich in history, architecture, and culinary delights, this charming hamlet has everything needed for a perfect UK getaway.

Cullen boasts a rich heritage dating back to the 12th century, with a boom in the fishing industry during the 18th century leading to the construction of iconic buildings that still stand today. Notable figures such as author David Macbeth Moir were born in the village, adding to its fascinating history.

The village's unique architecture is one of its standout features. Visitors can admire the Cullen House, a stunning 19th-century building, or take in the breathtaking views from the Cullen Viaduct. At the Cullen Square, visitors can explore local businesses or enjoy the bustling market.

No visit to Cullen would be complete without sampling the famous Cullen Skink soup. Made with smoked haddock, potatoes, onions, and cream, it is a hearty and warming dish that embodies Scottish cuisine and the village's fishing industry.

Cullen's strong sense of community is celebrated through annual events such as the Cullen Skink World Championships, the Cullen Gala, and the Cullen Car Rally. These traditions reflect the close-knit community spirit that makes Cullen a delightful place to reside in.

With its population of just over 1,400, Cullen offers an authentic small-town charm and the opportunity to escape the chaos of urban life. Visitors can enjoy relaxing on the village's sandy beaches or exploring the magnificent coastline.

In conclusion, Cullen is a village that offers a unique and enriching experience for visitors. With its enchanting history, stunning architecture, community spirit, and delicious cuisine, it's the perfect destination for those seeking a true taste of Scotland.

Dedham

Nestled ten miles northeast of Colchester lies the quaint village of Dedham in the scenic county of Essex. Rich in history dating back centuries, Dedham is a picture-perfect snapshot of English life complete with charming architecture, historical landmarks, and breathtaking countryside.

Perhaps the most notable symbol of Dedham is its association with the famous artist John Constable and the Dedham Vale. Born in the village in 1776, Constable was renowned for his romantic depictions of the British landscape, particularly the rolling hills and rivers of Dedham Vale, which served as a constant source of inspiration.

Spanning over Essex and Suffolk, the Dedham Vale is a designated Area of Outstanding Natural Beauty, characterized by green fields, winding streams, and tranquil hills. A stroll along the River Stour as it flows through Dedham's heart offers an unparalleled glimpse into Constable's stunning landscape paintings, making this historical hamlet a must-visit for any art enthusiast or nature lover.

Dedham has many historic landmarks to explore, including St Mary's Church, a Grade I listed structure dating back to the 15th century. A visit to Dedham Mill, operating since the 16th century, where the River Stour meets the Vale offers visitors a glimpse into Dedham's industrial past. The idyllic surroundings make it a perfect spot to take in the scenery and relax beside the flowing water.

A must-visit attraction is the Dedham Art & Craft Centre, situated in the historic Tannery. Local artisans display and sell their unique handmade pottery, jewelry, paintings, and textiles. Visitors can admire or purchase one-of-a-kind pieces while enjoying the quaint scenery.

Dedham is renowned for its warm community spirit, represented through unique customs, including the yearly Dedham Christmas Fair. The gathering features many festive stalls selling holiday trinkets, hot food, and mulled wine. Summer events such as the Dedham Music Festival celebrates both local and global talents, welcoming music lovers far and wide.

Surrounded by picturesque terrain, Dedham is a haven for outdoor enthusiasts. A network of walking and cycling paths, such as the Dedham Vale Way, welcomes visitors through the heart of the tranquil countryside. For seaside lovers, the village's close proximity to the coast provides opportunities for fishing or seashell hunting.

Falkland

Nestled in the charming countryside of Fife, Scotland, lies the enchanting village of Falkland. Renowned for its breathtaking appearance and fascinating past, this village has captured the hearts of many a history buff and Outlander fan alike. Join us as we journey through this captivating destination, featured in "100 Random Villages in the UK."

Falkland's history can be traced back to the 12th century when it was used as a royal hunting ground. It was later transformed into a magnificent estate, known as Falkland Palace, by the Earls of Fife in the 15th century. Home to the Scottish Stuart Dynasty and a favorite summer retreat for monarchs, it saw the famous "Union of the Crowns" negotiation between James VI of Scotland and Elizabeth I of England. Following restoration in the 19th and 20th centuries, visitors can now explore the nooks and crannies of this historical gem.

The Falkland Palace and Gardens is the crown jewel of the village, boasting architectural wonder and rich heritage. As a UNESCO World Heritage site, it features a remarkable collection of art and furniture, as well as a newly-renovated Royal Tennis Court. This iconic attraction has been used as a location in the popular show "Outlander," transporting viewers back to both the 1940s and 1960s. By day, visitors can witness the beauty of the Renaissance gardens and stunning architecture through daily tours.

Falkland has a tight-knit community that enjoys celebrating its heritage. The Falkland Apple Day, held in October, is dedicated to the harvest season and includes apple-themed activities such as juice pressing and live performances. The Falkland Craft Market, occurring on the first Saturday of each month, showcases handmade crafts, baked goods, and fresh produce from local artisans and traders.

Situated amidst the rolling hills of Fife, the Falkland village is enveloped in natural surroundings, with striking landscapes and verdant greenery. The nearby Lomond Hills Regional Park is a must-visit, with several nature trails catering to all levels of walkers, from leisurely walks to challenging hikes. Beautiful views of the picturesque countryside and its flora and fauna await.

With its thriving community and romantic charm, Falkland continues to be a draw for those seeking a tranquil retreat. Visitors can explore the quaint cobbled streets lined with charming shops displaying local artwork and heritage foods. Alternatively, they can indulge in Scotland's traditional cuisine at cozy taverns such as The Bruce Inn. For those looking to prolong their stay, picturesque B&Bs and rental cottages provide a comfortable and rustic experience.

Guiting Power

Nestled in the quaint Cotswolds of England, Guiting Power is a picturesque village that exudes tranquility and charm with its traditional Cotswold architecture and serene rural setting. As we embark on a journey to explore this charming village, we shall unearth its numerous landmarks, cultural sites, geographical features, unique traditions, and community activities, which have earned it a spot among the 100 Random Villages in the UK.

The rich history of Guiting Power dates back to the 15th century, and it was once a thriving market town. It still boasts of notable historical figures like John Masefield and William Morris, who lived in the village's manor house. During the 19th century, it was known for wool production, and today, the village is known for its landmarks and cultural sites.

St. Michael's and All Angels Church is the village's most remarkable landmark, with its beautiful Norman tower and stained-glass windows. The church, built in the 12th century, has an interior decorated with intricate carvings and sculptures. Other cultural sites worth a visit include the village's local pub, the Farmers Arms, which is over 400 years old. With delicious food and drink, it offers a taste of traditional British cuisine.

Guiting Festival celebrates the village's music, food, and culture annually, showcasing the community's unique traditions and spirit. It also features a traditional Cotswold Morris Dancing performance, which involves colorful costumes and lively music. The Christmas market held in the village's town hall is another fantastic community activity where stalls sell handmade crafts, gifts, and festive foods.

Guiting Power is located in an area of outstanding natural beauty, making it a paradise for nature enthusiasts. Rolling hills, meandering rivers, and lush forests surround the village, offering ample opportunities for outdoor activities like walking and cycling. The Guiting Woods, located just outside the village, is a great place to explore nature, and the Bluebell Walk is a must-visit during springtime when the forest is carpeted with vibrant bluebells.

Guiting Power's community is friendly and welcoming, and the weekly farmers' market sells locally sourced produce, meat, and dairy products, highlighting the village's current aspects of life. Its unique charm, rich history, culture, and beautiful landscape make Guiting Power an ideal destination for history buffs, nature enthusiasts, and foodies alike.

Hathersage

Nestled in the northern part of Derbyshire, Hathersage is a charming village that has been a beloved destination for centuries. Whether it's the breathtaking natural landscapes, rich heritage, literary legacy, or exciting outdoor activities, Hathersage has it all. The village is a celebrated location linked to Charlotte Brontë's famous novel "Jane Eyre," as well as a host of striking landmarks and cultural sites. Let's delve into the village's fascinating history, natural surrounds, and modern-day aspects to discover why Hathersage is such a unique and captivating location.

Hathersage's history dates back to the Roman period, with an ancient road believed to have run through the village. The thriving medieval period saw the introduction of lead mining and farming, which bolstered the community. During the late 18th century, the village was the residence of the renowned adventurer and botanist Joseph Banks, who played a pivotal role in James Cook's first voyage to Australia. Today, Hathersage is a vibrant village that honors its rich history through its monuments and cultural sites.

One of these significant landmarks is the Church of St Michael and All Angels, showcasing incredible architecture that includes a Norman chancel arch, Gothic tower, and 16th-century transepts. The churchyard is also home to the grave of Little John, Robin Hood's loyal sidekick. The village's Outdoor Pool is another must-visit attraction, surrounded by awe-inspiring scenery. Featured in movies such as "The Other Boleyn Girl" and "Pride and Prejudice," the heated pool provides an unforgettable experience. Hathersage is also famous for North Lees Hall, credited with inspiring Charlotte Brontë's depiction of Thornfield Hall in "Jane Eyre."

Hathersage is a bustling village with a close-knit community that delights in celebrating its unique traditions. One such notable event is Bonnie Prince Charlie Day, which is celebrated annually on 10th May, commemorating the failed Jacobite Rising of 1745. The Millstones Fell Race, taking place every August bank holiday Monday, is also a popular activity, attracting adventurers from all over the UK with its six-mile course through the moorland, trails, and bogs.

Nestled in the heart of the Peak District National Park, Hathersage captivates with its stunning natural environs, diverse wildlife, and splendorous landscapes. Stanage Edge, renowned as a world-class climbing spot, offers sensational views of the Dark Peak moorland. The village provides access to exhilarating hikes, from the Bamford Edge to Hathersage Moor and Burbage Edge. The River Derwent, flowing through the village, is perfect for fishing and canoeing.

Kettlewell

Nestled in the gorgeous Yorkshire Dales, Kettlewell is a rustic village that beckons locals and tourists alike with its historic charm, verdant surroundings and lively community. Featured in the blockbuster "Calendar Girls", Kettlewell is fast becoming a go-to destination in the UK. This article delineates some of the reasons why Kettlewell has so much appeal.

Kettlewell's history dates back far beyond the Roman period, as evidenced by the discovery of an impressive Roman settlement nearby. Wool trade passed down for centuries dominated the village economy for a long time. Not only St. Mary's Church, built in the 12th century and famous for its breathtaking stained-glass windows, circular font, and a spectacular three-tiered Jacobean pulpit, but a row of iconic stone cottages known as Nutter's Houses also hold a special place in the village's history.

Apart from its architectural and historical significance, Kettlewell is renowned for its thriving cultural scene. The art exhibition is a favourite among art lovers, where local artists display their stunning works. The Kettlewell Scarecrow Festival and the annual Christmas Fair come with their charm as well. During these events, visitors can see custom-made scarecrows displaying local traditions and purchase festive goodies and handmade crafts.

Located in the heart of the Yorkshire Dales, Kettlewell boasts picturesque natural surroundings, including rolling hills, moorlands, and tranquil waterways. Visitors can explore the area either on foot, bike, or even on horseback, with several trails and paths providing easy access to the stunning landscape. Besides, the thriving local wildlife, including roe deer, red squirrels, and many bird species, is breathtaking.

Kettlewell boasts a vibrant community that is the heart of this charming village. The community works hand in hand to hold fundraising events and participate in local traditions, ensuring that the village's hospitality, warmth, and camaraderie extend to all visitors. The village is home to a range of delightful shops, welcoming pubs, and friendly faces, which visitors can experience by staying in one of the many guesthouses or vacation rentals.

In short, Kettlewell is a village that captivates visitors with its rich history, unique cultural traditions, stunning natural landscapes, and warm community life. It's a place where local communities, enthusiasts, and tourists with an interest in authentic British life will find much to savour. So why not plan a trip today to bask in the unspoilt beauty of one of Britain's most alluring villages?

Lacock

Nestled in the heart of Wiltshire is Lacock – a charming and idyllic village that has stood the test of time for over a thousand years. Steeped in history, it's a place that exudes classic charm and natural beauty. The cobbled streets, medieval architecture, and rolling countryside provide a picturesque backdrop that's hard to resist.

One of the village's most notable landmarks is Lacock Abbey, a sprawling estate that's been standing tall over the land since the 13th century The grandeur and history of the Abbey is undeniable; it has been a place of significance to the film industry, serving as a backdrop for iconic movies such as "Harry Potter." A rich facet of the village's identity includes William Henry Fox Talbot, a photography pioneer who was a former resident of the grand estate. Visitors can experience a slice of the heritage of Lacock Abbey, with guided tours open to the public.

The Tithe Barn is another cultural gem that deserves mention, an impressive structure that dates back to the 14th century. What was once a grain storage unit is now a popular venue for weddings, musical concerts, and other cultural festivities.

Lacock is a village of strong community spirit, with plenty of local traditions and activities to discover. During the festive season, the village comes alive with holiday cheer, with carol singers, festive stalls, and local delicacies on offer. The Lacock Players, a local drama group, add their contribution to the community with regular productions showcasing contemporary adaptations and classic plays. Different clubs and groups catering to different interests abound, bringing everyone together.

But the crown jewel of Lacock is the lure of the natural surroundings – that peaceful respite from the hustle and bustle of city life. The village is famous for its rolling hills, picturesque meadows, and the tranquil River Avon that cuts across the stunning countryside. Visitors can take refreshing walks and explore the natural surroundings, while marvelous attractions such as Stonehenge and the vibrant city of Bath are easily accessible.

Lacock is a vibrant community with a welcoming local population. The village is home to a well-stocked village shop and post office, with a charming pub serving up a cozy atmosphere. For travel enthusiasts, Lacock should be the top choice on their list of 100 random villages to visit in the UK. The village's friendly residents, stunning natural scenery, and rich history combine to make Lacock a magnet for visitors and a delightful place to live.

Lower Slaughter

Nestled in the heart of the Cotswolds, Lower Slaughter is a gem of a village that radiates an undeniable sense of peace and tranquility. Its natural beauty remains untouched, and the meandering River Eye that flows through the village serves as the perfect allure for visitors from all over the world. A trip to Lower Slaughter promises a journey of exploring the Cotswold charm in its undisturbed state, providing a sense of relaxation and simplicity that is hard to come by in our modern world.

Lower Slaughter boasts of a rich history dating back to pre-Roman times, and during the Roman period, the village was renowned for its textile industry. In the Middle Ages, the wool trade flourished, making the village home to several well-to-do wool merchants. The village boasts of iconic historical figures such as Sir Max Beerbohm, a renowned artist and caricaturist, whose family lived in the village. Sir Herbert Beerbohm Tree, a Shakespearean actor and theater impresario, was Sir Max Beerbohm's brother, and the village maintains a connection to William Morris, the founder of the Arts and Crafts movement, who lived in Chipping Campden, a nearby town.

The village's 19th-century cottages and medieval buildings give it a timeless charm, with the 13th-century church of St. Mary being the most notable landmark at its heart. The Old Mill, built in the 18th century, sits on the shoulder of the River Eye, now serving as a museum that showcases the traditional textile production methods that made this village renowned.

Despite being a tourist hotspot, the village's locals place a strong emphasis on tradition, hosting an annual Flower and Vegetable Show that celebrates the beauty of horticulture and community spirit. The village also has an active history group that conducts walking tours to help visitors explore the rich history of the village. The village's unique businesses, like the Slaughters Country Inn, offer luxury accommodation and top-notch dining in the heart of the countryside, while the Mill Shop houses collections of woolen products produced by local weavers.

Lower Slaughter's natural surroundings are impossible to ignore, with the crystal-clear waters of the River Eye home to trout and other aquatic life, making it an ideal spot for angling and picnicking. The village is surrounded by tranquil meadows, rolling hills, and lush green fields, perfect for a leisurely walk or a stroll to Upper Slaughter, the neighboring village.

Although Lower Slaughter has become a tourist attraction, it continues to embody charm and elegance, with modern amenities while retaining its natural elegance. The village community is gracious, ensuring the visitor always feels at home.

Orford

Nestled on the charming east coast of Suffolk, Orford is a quaint village that oozes character and history. It's no wonder this destination is loved by tourists and locals alike. With its wonky clock tower peeking over the main street, unique independent shops, and traditional fishing community, there is something about Orford that will pull visitors in. However, it's the village's rich history that really sets it apart.

Orford Castle is without question one of the village's most significant landmarks. Built by King Henry II in the 12th century, the castle played a role in the lookout strategy for the King's fleet during the reign of Richard the Lionheart. Nowadays, the castle is known for its rare keep - a medieval rarity in England. Standing at over 27 meters in height, the keep's walls are over 3 meters thick, making it an awe-inspiring sight to behold.

The castle wasn't the only residence for powerful figures in Orford - Eleanor of Aquitaine had the misfortune of being imprisoned here for several months in the 14th century. King Henry II's wife was accused of aiding her son's revolt against his father and was deemed enough of a threat to be imprisoned. Her imprisonment ended when Edward I claimed the castle for himself.

While powerful figures have certainly left their mark on Orford, the village also has a long tradition of community spirit that can be seen in its fishing industry. The village has long relied on fishing, specifically for oysters, which have been harvested in nearby Butley Creek since Roman times. Although the oyster beds are now closed for conservation purposes, family-run businesses, such as Barretts, Richardson's Smokehouse, and Pinney's of Orford, continue the fishing heritage of the village.

Aside from its landmarks and fishing industry, Orford is a haven for nature lovers and architecture buffs. The quirky Norman Church of St. Bartholomew's with its stone quarry-tiled floor is a must-visit. The Orford Ness, a shingle spit that juts into the North Sea, has a fascinating history as the testing site for the UK's top-secret atomic weapons during the Cold War. Bird-watchers and walkers will fall in love with the stunning coastline, marshes and surrounding nature.

Orford is a close-knit community with no shortage of activities or events to keep residents and visitors entertained. The Orford Town Trust oversees several community initiatives and events throughout the year, from an annual fête to open gardens. During the summer months, visitors can explore pop-up stalls offering delicious treats, crafts, and trinkets.

Painswick

As you explore the winding streets and verdant landscapes of Painswick, you'll feel as if you've stepped into a storybook world. This picturesque Cotswold village is brimming with character and charm, from its rolling hills to its quaint shops and cafes. It's easy to see why Painswick has become a must-visit destination for travelers seeking the authentic English experience.

The history of Painswick is as fascinating as it is varied. In the 15th century, the village was a hub of the wool trade, with a thriving market that attracted merchants from far and wide. Later, Painswick became a center for religious dissent, with Nonconformists and Quakers calling it home. Today, the village's rich history is still visible in its ancient buildings and landmarks.

Perhaps the most unique of these landmarks is the Rococo Garden, an 18th-century masterpiece that offers visitors a glimpse into a bygone era. The garden's maze, grotto, and follies are sure to delight visitors of all ages. Another must-see attraction is the Painswick Church, with its famous yew trees that are both eerie and beautiful.

Despite its ancient roots, Painswick is a thriving community that offers modern amenities and conveniences. You'll find excellent schools and housing options, along with plenty of local businesses that contribute to the area's spirit. The village hosts an annual arts festival and a Christmas street fair that provides a taste of the village's warm community spirit.

But perhaps the best thing about Painswick is its natural beauty. Surrounded by the stunning Cotswold Hills, the village boasts a plethora of walking routes and trails that offer breathtaking views. Take a stroll up to the Beacon Tower and soak in the panoramic vistas – you'll never forget the view.

In conclusion, Painswick is a treasure trove of history, culture, and adventure. Whether you're a local or a visitor, there's always something new to discover in this charming English village. Come and explore – you won't regret it.

Robin Hood's Bay

Nestled on the rocky coast of North Yorkshire, lies the charming village of Robin Hood's Bay. With a rich history in smuggling and breathtaking natural landscapes, it's easy to see why this hidden gem is the perfect destination for those seeking an escape.

Rooted back to the Bronze Age, Robin Hood's Bay didn't become a hub for smuggling activity until the 16th century. With its secluded location and hidden alleys, it was the ideal place for smugglers to bring contraband without detection. Infamous smugglers such as Francis Leyland and William Thompson created a fascinating history that's still felt throughout the village today. Traditional fishermen's cottages, old pubs, and cobbled streets create a charming, historic atmosphere.

Visitors can't miss the dramatic coastline marked by towering cliffs, rugged headlands with quaint fishing boats bobbing in the harbour. Landmarks that showcase the village's history include the Old Coastguard Station and the Robin Hood's Bay Methodist Chapel that date back to the 19th century.

Robin Hood's Bay's vibrant community hosts a range of traditional events throughout the year. Visitors can enjoy the annual village fair and watch local children dress up as beavers and parade through the streets during the Baytown Beavers Day. The village also has many unique businesses such as quirky cafes, independent shops selling handmade crafts, and traditional fishmongers where you can buy fresh catch straight from the North Sea.

The stunning landscapes that surround Robin Hood's Bay offer visitors a chance to explore the natural wonders of the area. The scenic Cleveland Way hiking trail winds along the clifftops above the sea, providing an ideal space to spot wildlife such as seabirds nesting in the cliffs or seals basking on the rocks.

Whether you're a history buff, a nature lover, or simply looking for a charming seaside escape, Robin Hood's Bay has something to offer. Its past and unique traditions add to its appeal, while its dramatic coastline and stunning landscapes form the perfect backdrop for exploring the great outdoors. With a warm, welcoming community and a wealth of local businesses, it's easy to see how this small village has become such a beloved destination for both visitors and residents.

Shere

Shere is a breath-taking village located in the heart of Surrey Hills. It is a gem that showcases the beauty and charm of rural England. A visit to Shere promises to be an unforgettable experience that offers a harmonious blend of natural beauty, history, and culture.

With its quaint streets, majestic buildings, and prominence in film appearances, Shere epitomizes the idyllic English village life. It is a cornerstone of Middle Ages history and an important trading stop between London and Portsmouth. Remarkable figures and events like James Oglethorpe and the English Civil War add to the village's rich history.

Furthermore, the village boasts of a plethora of historical landmarks, including St. James's Church and the White Horse Inn pub, which has been a local watering hole for centuries. For those with a passion for museums, the Shere Museum is an excellent destination to explore the village's intriguing history.

Shere is not only an excellent historical destination, but it's also popular within the film industry worldwide. Its charming and picturesque streetscapes have been used as a location for movies like Bridget Jones: The Edge of Reason and The Holiday.

Shere's community spirit speaks volumes about the kindliness of the residents. It is evident through popular events like the Shere Village Fair, which has been a tradition for over a century, and the Shere Hill Climb, an event that car enthusiasts from all over the UK eagerly anticipate. The community center is also alive with a wide range of activities that cater to people of all ages.

What's more, Shere is located in one of the most scenic areas of the UK. With vast countryside views, nature lovers can explore the beautiful walking and cycling trails and take in the stunning views of the Surrey Hills.

In summary, Shere is a destination that has something for everyone. Whether you have a passion for history, nature, or culture, this village provides a perfect opportunity to experience the best of rural England. Make sure it's a must-visit destination on your wish list for a unique and unforgettable travel experience.

Staithes

Nestled along the coast of North Yorkshire, the charming village of Staithes is a must-visit destination for anyone looking for an authentic English village with a rich maritime history. With its red-roofed cottages and quaint cobbled streets, Staithes offers a fascinating glimpse into the country's seafaring past, as well as cultural attractions for tourists and locals alike.

Dating back to the medieval era, Staithes is steeped in history. Back then, it was a bustling port for the local alum and ironstone trades. However, it wasn't until the 18th century when the village became a fishing town, and its population began to grow rapidly. It was during this period that a young apprentice named James Cook came to report on the village for his employer, a local merchant. Cook was immediately taken with the town's bustling harbor, and he would return to Staithes again and again over the years. To this day, visitors can learn more about the village's maritime heritage and Captain Cook's connection to the area at the Captain Cook Museum, which houses a collection of personal items and artifacts from the explorer's life.

Aside from its rich history, Staithes also offers visitors stunning natural surroundings. The village is surrounded by towering cliffs to the north and the vast expanse of the North Sea to the south, making it the perfect destination for outdoor enthusiasts. Staithes lies within the North York Moors National Park, an area characterized by breathtaking moorland vistas, rolling hills, and ancient woodlands that provide endless opportunities for hiking and exploring.

Visitors to Staithes can also discover some of the village's unique landmarks, such as Cowbar Nab, a narrow geological formation featured in BBC's hit TV series 'Dracula'. Composed of distinctive layers of shales and sands that have eroded over time to create a dramatic landscape, this natural landmark is a popular destination for hikers and nature enthusiasts.

Staithes is a village that prides itself on its community spirit and commitment to preserving its rich heritage. Visitors can participate in activities such as guided walks, storytelling sessions, and craft workshops that offer a chance to learn more about the village's cultural traditions. They can also explore independent shops, galleries, and historic pubs selling local goods, crafts, and excellent seafood.

Today, Staithes is a thriving community that welcomes visitors from all over the world who come to experience the village's unique charm and breathtaking natural setting. It's a must-visit destination for those interested in exploring maritime history, hiking the rugged North Yorkshire coast, or simply relaxing with a pint at a lively local pub.

Tissington

Tissington, nestled in the picturesque Derbyshire Dales, is a charming village with a history that dates back to pre-Roman times. This quaint village has become a destination for travelers and history enthusiasts due to its well-dressing traditions and historical hall. The 17th-century Tissington Hall, built under the ownership of Earl Ferrers, has been the most significant landmark of the village. The village also played a vital role in the agricultural revolution of the 18th and 19th centuries.

Apart from Tissington Hall, the village's most significant landmark, the village is famous for its well-dressing traditions that have been traced back over 700 years. During summer, the village comes alive with colorful displays of well-dressed wells, each depicting a different theme. It is a celebration of Tissington's natural beauty and history. The village is renowned for its tight-knit community and traditional values reflected in the many events and festivals such as the Tissington Candlemas Pancake Races and Tissington Pumpkin Trail.

Tissington is set in the heart of the Peak District National Park, so there are plenty of opportunities to explore the surrounding landscapes, including rolling hills, lush green meadows, and dazzling wildflowers. It is the perfect place for outdoor activities like hiking, cycling, rock climbing, and pony trekking.

The thriving local businesses, including artisan bakeries, breweries, antique shops, and art galleries, contribute to Tissington's unique character. Visitors can explore these local businesses and take a piece of Tissington home with them.

The village offers a peaceful and tranquil setting, perfect for residents who want to live a charming and idyllic way of life away from the hustle and bustle of the city. It is a popular destination for tourists drawn to the well-dressing traditions and Tissington Hall yet retains its authentic, traditional character. Tissington is a hidden gem of the English countryside that captures the essence of a bygone era. A trip to this village is a chance to connect with the past, enjoy the present, and take in the stunning natural beauty that surrounds the place.

Welldale

The rolling hills of the Yorkshire Dales shelter a hidden treasure – Welldale, a postcard-worthy village that captivates visitors with its pristine landscapes. Whether you are a history enthusiast or an outdoor lover, this slice of British countryside will delight you with its charm.

The ancient village traces its roots back to the 16th century and has been a source of inspiration for Sarah Harrison, a celebrated Yorkshire poet, whose masterpieces were crafted here. The unassuming locals take immense pride in their heritage, and the village's rich history is palpable from every nook and corner.

At the heart of the village lies St. Mary's Church – a magnificent Gothic building that dates back to the 12th century. The grandeur of the architecture is unmatched, and the church's walls echo with stories of the past, inviting visitors to unravel its secrets.

However, the village's most captivating landmark is its own waterfall, tucked within the York Moors national park. This picturesque natural wonder has been a hub of attraction for centuries, drawing visitors from far and wide. The stunning cascade is a symphony of colours, music, and the beauty of nature.

Welldale's quaint countryside is home to a welcoming and hospitable community with a vibrant local culture. Visitors can experience the village's character by sipping a pint or relishing traditional Yorkshire dishes at one of the many local pubs, feeling right at home.

The breathtaking Yorkshire Dales offer miles of winding trails for outdoor adventurers, offering glimpses of some of the UK's most beautiful landscapes. And for birdwatchers, the area's lush woodlands and rolling hills provide a perfect habitat for a plethora of bird species.

Welldale is a village that carries its rich past into its modern-day life. The locals' warm and friendly nature adds to the village's magic, and visitors will find themselves hooked from the moment they arrive. The village presents the ideal blend of history, culture, and natural beauty, making it one of the UK's best-kept secrets.

Zennor

Nestled within the rolling hills of West Cornwall, you'll uncover the beguiling village of Zennor. Filled with legends, folklore, and a rich history that will transport you to bygone eras, it's no wonder that Zennor is regarded as one of the UK's hidden gems. In this chapter, we'll take you on a journey through the magic and wonder of Zennor. From its myths, including the fabled Mermaid of Zennor, to its awe-inspiring rugged landscapes, we'll reveal all the reasons why you should add Zennor to your adventure list.

The village has stood the test of time, with inhabitants that date back to prehistoric times. During the early Middle Ages, Zennor was a hub for trade and commerce due to its proximity to the sea, which made it a favorable location for fishermen and sailors. Celtic monks founded a priory that soon became a major center for religious activity in the area. As time passed, Zennor became known for its prosperous mining industries and today, it's praised for its thriving artistic community.

As you wander through Zennor, you'll discover hidden treasures full of stories and vibrant culture. The Mermaid of Zennor is one of its most renowned legends, and visitors can follow the Mermaid Trail to learn about locations central to the story. The 12th-century Church of St. Senara is a significant landmark with its ornate carvings and stunning stained glass windows. A short distance away, the iconic Zennor Quoit will transport you back in time to the days of standing stones.

Despite having fewer than 200 inhabitants, Zennor bursts with energy and life. Traditional pubs and local businesses, run by friendly locals, are refreshingly authentic. The Tinners Arms, a charming old pub, is a local favorite, and Churchtown Farmhouse, a quaint tearoom in the heart of the village, serves some of the most exquisite scones and clotted cream in Cornwall. Every July, the village kicks off the Plen-an-Gwari festival, with music, dance, and performances, all staged in the village's ancient amphitheater.

The diverse natural surroundings and landscapes of Zennor showcase its rugged beauty. Following the South-West Coast Path offers breathtaking views of the village and its surroundings. On your walk, you'll discover ancient stone circles, striking cliffs, and vast farmland. A paradise for nature lovers, you may even spot the rare Cornish Chough bird.

Zennor's sense of community spirit is reflected in its abundance of modern vitality. While steeped in history, it's very much alive with a vibrant arts scene, frequent galleries, workshops, and exhibitions. During the festive period, the village hall is transformed into a winter wonderland for the annual Zennor Christmas Tree Festival.

Bibury

The picturesque village of Bibury in Gloucestershire, England, is just the kind of place that grabs your attention with its natural beauty and rich history. Its name, "Bibury," was derived from "Bibra's Farm," and the village dates back to the Roman era. But Bibury's real draw is its iconic Arlington Row cottages, Grade I listed buildings that have been featured on UK currency, movies, and TV shows, and are a must-see attraction that draws visitors from around the world.

The cottages were built in the 17th century as weavers' cottages and are constructed from local stone with steeply pitched roofs covered with Cotswold stone tiles. Today, they serve as a reminder of the village's rich history and provide a fascinating glimpse into its past. Bibury is also home to St. Mary's, a 14th-century church that features stained-glass windows and a Norman font. Guided tours of the church are available, allowing visitors to explore its history and learn more about the village's heritage.

But Bibury's charm extends beyond its historic buildings. The village boasts a central river, the River Coln, and numerous walking paths throughout the village and wider countryside that enable visitors to soak up the beauty of the Cotswold landscape. Its peaceful surroundings provide a perfect spot to relax and enjoy the scenery.

Bibury also has a strong sense of community, and local businesses such as tea rooms and gift shops contribute to the economy and enhance the village's character. Every June, the village hosts an annual fete that brings together villagers and visitors in a celebration of the area's rich history and culture.

Bibury is also known for its connection to Catherine of Aragon, the wife of King Henry VIII. Catherine stayed at the nearby Calcot Manor when she first arrived in England and is thought to have visited Bibury during her time there.

This, alongside its quaint cottages, ancient church, and bewitching natural surroundings, has made Bibury one of the most beautiful and picturesque villages in the UK, attracting visitors from all around the world.

Blanchland

Nestled amongst the idyllic North Pennines Area of Outstanding Natural Beauty, Blanchland is the epitome of a perfect medieval village. Its origins date back to the 12th century when a group of French monks established a monastery at the very spot where the village stands today. Since then, Blanchland has remained an immaculately preserved conservation area, a place where visitors can experience authentic medieval life.

The village's history is full of fascinating details that transport visitors back in time. The founding of Blanchland Monastery in the 1160s by French monks fostered a thriving community until it was dissolved under King Henry VIII in the 16th century. The village has since passed through various hands until the Bishop of Durham purchased it in 1709. It remained in the Bishop's family until Marjorie Crew, the last owner, gifted the village to the National Trust in 1961.

Today, Blanchland is a treasure trove of key landmarks and cultural sites. The medieval ruins of the Benedictine abbey remain the most arresting architectural feature in the village. The abbey, partially destroyed during the dissolution of the monasteries, is now a registered ancient monument. Another sight to behold is the Inn, originally built as a dwelling for the Bishop's agent in the 18th century, and now an inn with a distinctive pink façade and white window frames.

Blanchland's parish church of St. Mary the Virgin was initially run by the monks but rebuilt in the 19th century under the commission of Nathaniel Crewe. It hosts unique artifacts and a rare barrel-vaulted ceiling for visitors to admire. The annual May Day celebrations have been a village tradition for over a century, where locals and visitors gather to watch the raising of the maypole and celebrate the arrival of spring.

The village is also home to remarkable local businesses, including a blacksmith's forge, artisanal shops, a bakery, farm shop, and tearooms. Blanchland's natural surroundings of hills and forests make it an excellent base for exploring the North Pennines. The nearby Derwent Reservoir provides stunning views and excellent fishing opportunities, while the surrounding moors have miles of scenic footpaths to explore.

Blanchland is a bustling hub of community life, with various local clubs and groups that connect residents and offer plenty of opportunities to experience village life. It attracts many tourists wanting to experience authentic medieval life and adds to Blanchland's vibrancy, making it a must-visit destination in the UK.

Castle Acre

As you roam the heart of Norfolk, you're bound to come across the quaint and charming village of Castle Acre. This village reverberates through time, taking you back to the Norman conquest of England. With ruins of the Castle Acre Priory, Castle Acre village tells the tales of its fascinating past.

The late 11th century saw Castle Acre come under William de Warenne, a trusted advisor to William the Conqueror. It quickly became a powerful centre in the region with the construction of the Castle Acre Castle, which stands tall as a testament to Norman military architecture.

Castle Acre Priory, founded by Warenne in 1090, was one of the largest and most important monasteries in Norfolk. A home to the thriving monks' community, they built a grand church and numerous outbuildings. This led to the village's growth as a bustling market town and trading centre for wool and cloth in the 14th and 15th centuries. Even today, the village retains a historic character with many original buildings standing around, revelling in the glorious past.

The Castle Acre village offers a striking picture with the ruins of Castle Acre Priory being the most prominent feature. It was dissolved in 1537 by Henry VIII, and later converted into a grand country house. Tourists are free to wander the ruins of the priory, marvel at the intricate stonework and imagine living in its glory days. Castle Acre Castle is another landmark worth visiting - its keep and curtain walls still standing tall.

The All Saints Church, a marvel built in the 12th century, displays beautiful stained-glass windows, a Norman font, and a wrought-iron bell cage, giving it an otherworldly feel. The Castle Acre Morris Men group has preserved the unique English Morris dancing for the village, and they perform at festivals and events regularly. The village also hosts an annual summer fete complete with music, games, and locally-sourced food and drink.

Castle Acre is surrounded by lush greenery and stunning countryside. There are numerous walking and cycling routes in the area, including the long-distance walking trail of Peddars Way that goes through the village. As you explore, you'll witness the tranquil River Nar running through Castle Acre and the nearby Castle Acre Common that is home to a variety of rare plants and wildlife.

Castle Acre is a true gem of Norfolk that every traveller should add to their bucket list. With a natural beauty so serene and history so rich, this village is bound to leave you enchanted. Whether it's walking through nature, browsing boutiques, or savouring artisanal bakery treats from The Gingerbread House, Castle Acre has it all.

Dent

Nestled amidst the picturesque rolling hills of the Yorkshire Dales lies Dent, a quaint village of rich heritage and cultural significance. As one of the delightful villages featured in "100 Random Villages in the UK", Dent has much to offer its visitors in terms of historical charm and natural beauty.

Dating back to the Industrial Revolution, the village has a strong association with wool production and is particularly renowned for its impressive 'Terrible Knitters'. These gifted women gained notoriety during the Second World War for their less-than-perfect knitting, a deliberate strategy to prevent the item being sent to the harsh conditions of the Russian front.

Stroll along the cobbled streets, steeped in history and intrigue and one is immediately struck by the sense of character and charm that keeps visitors coming back year after year. These age-old pathways were constructed by prisoners of war during the Napoleonic Wars, and each stone holds a unique story, lending an intriguing dimension to the village's past.

For those seeking a deeper insight into the village's cultural heritage, Dent Heritage Centre offers an immersive experience of the area's traditional practices of farming and wool production. Visitors will be captivated by the intricacy of the 12th-century St. Andrew's Church, boasting exquisite carvings and stained-glass windows.

As well as being steeped in history, Dent is surrounded by natural beauty, with delightful valleys and serene streams perfect for the avid hiker or nature enthusiast. Admire the stunning scenery alongside the delightful sounds of singing birds and take a deep breath of the sweet mountain air.

With a lively sense of community that thrives on tradition, Dent is a modern village that is proud of its cultural roots. From the annual Dent Music and Beer Festival, which draws visitors to the picturesque village from far and wide, to the local Dent Brewery and Village Shop, which remain vital parts of the town's thriving economy, the character and charm of Dent is alive and well.

In conclusion, Dent is a truly unique village, with a rich history, a captivating cultural heritage and breathtaking natural beauty. Visit the village for an unforgettable vacation or make this charming community your home and enjoy the sense of community spirit that remains very much alive and well in this delightful corner of the UK.

Eyam

Nestled in the hilly landscape of Derbyshire, England, lies a small village called Eyam. This village is an embodiment of courage and resilience as it self-quarantined during the devastating Plague of 1665 that brought death and hysteria throughout the country. Despite having a population of only 350 people, the villagers made the painful decision to close themselves off from the outside world to prevent the spread of the disease. This act of heroism impressed many and has been seen as a shining example of the community coming together in times of need.

The tragedy began when a tailor named George Viccars received a parcel of contaminated cloth from London, introducing the bubonic plague into the village. However, the villagers didn't stand idly by and wait for death to take them. Under the guidance of their rector, William Mompesson, and Puritan minister, Thomas Stanley, the village took drastic measures. They erected a boundary stone to mark the perimeter, negotiated supply deliveries with neighbouring villages, and set up a pest house to quarantine the infected. They also worked together to bury their dead, with a mortality rate of over 70%.

Eyam is home to several key landmarks and cultural sites that showcase its rich history. One site that stands out is the Plague Cottages containing the remains of the first three plague victims. Other noteworthy landmarks include St. Lawrence Church, Eyam Museum, and Eyam Hall, a beautiful Elizabethan manor that has been in the Wright family for over 300 years.

The village holds an annual Plague Sunday Service at St. Lawrence Church to honour those who passed during the epidemic. Additionally, residents plant "plague bulbs" along the funeral procession routes of the victims. Visitors can indulge in cakes and homemade scones at the charming Eyam Tea Rooms, shop locally sourced yarn at Eyam Yarns, and taste local craft beer at Eyam Real Ale Company.

Eyam is located within the Peak District National Park, offering visitors stunning views of the surrounding countryside. The "Plague Walk" is a self-guided tour along the funeral procession routes of the plague victims that showcases the region's natural beauty.

Today, Eyam is a vibrant and welcoming community with a strong sense of pride in its history and traditions. Local businesses provide employment opportunities, and the village holds several events throughout the year, such as the Eyam Well Dressing Festival. In short, Eyam is a unique and charming village that embodies resilience, history, and stunning landscapes.

Finchingfield

Nestled in the heart of scenic Essex, Finchingfield is a village that is often regarded as one of the most beautiful places in all of England. Its picturesque green and tranquil pond are undeniably one of the village's most attractive features. With charming, idyllic scenery, visitors to Finchingfield can expect to experience the best of the English countryside.

Finchingfield's history can be traced all the way back to the Domesday Book in 1086 when it was known as 'Fincingfelda.' In more recent times, it is renowned for Radclyffe Hall, who lived in the village during the early part of the 20th century and penned novel after novel, including 'The Well of Loneliness.'

The village is home to many notable landmarks which provide an insight into its history. Among the standout buildings is the stunning Church of St. John the Baptist, which dates back to the 15th century and boasts some of the finest medieval stained-glass windows in the country. Visitors can marvel at the oldest complete set of change-ringing bells in England atop the church tower.

The red-brick Windmill, evidence of Finchingfield's rich farming heritage, offers a unique glimpse into village life as it was in the early 19th century. And, serving as a center of trade in the 15th century, the Finchingfield Guildhall is now a museum, showcasing the village's rich textile legacy.

Finchingfield's unique traditions and local businesses are an integral aspect of village life. The annual Finchingfield Flower Festival held every June, sees the church and several of the village's homes decorated with stunning floral displays, and visitors can enjoy traditional local delicacies and crafts. Its vibrant community spirit sees locals coming together to create a thriving local economy, with everything from freshly baked goods to traditional pubs.

Standing out against its competitors, Finchingfield's stunning green and picturesque pond are phenomenal. Surrounded by ancient cottages and oak trees, it is a perfect place for afternoon walks, fishing trips, or for simply taking in the majestic ambiance. For those who love hiking, the village is also a great starting point to explore the rolling hills and picture-perfect villages that are synonymous with England's countryside.

Today, Finchingfield remains a bustling community, and visitors looking for the best accommodations can find top-quality bed and breakfast spots. For those looking to relocate, the village has a welcoming community, excellent schools, and easy access to the nearby cities of Cambridge and London.

Hawkshead

Nestled in Cumbria's picturesque countryside, the charming village of Hawkshead boasts rich historical roots, making it a perfect entry in "100 Random Villages in the UK". Having thrived as a prosperous wool market town in the 12th century, it eventually surrendered to the waning textile industry in the 19th century. Nevertheless, it preserved its historic buildings and is a veritable time capsule that beams with antiquity.

Notably, world-renowned poet William Wordsworth and beloved author Beatrix Potter lived in Hawkshead during different periods of their lives, earning it a reputation as a haven for literature enthusiasts.

The Old Grammar School is a fascinating landmark that beckons history buffs. Completed in 1585, it is where Wordsworth honed his classic writing style. Hawkshead's central square is another key attraction, paved with cobblestones and lined with ancient buildings that serve as a backdrop to the village's lively community activities and unique traditions.

St. Michael's and All Angels is an impressive church from the 16th century that boasts dazzling stained-glass windows. And if you're an ardent Potterite, then a visit to Beatrix Potter Gallery is a must. Housed in a 17th-century former solicitor's office, the gallery showcases a vast collection of the author's illustrations.

Hawkshead's natural surroundings are an ideal destination for avid walkers and hikers looking to bask in the Nehruvian countryside. Lake Windermere, the largest lake in England, is a short drive away and provides a perfect base for exploring the surrounding fells and scenic forests. The Grizedale Forest is home to several wildlife treasures, including red squirrels, deer, and even ospreys during summer.

Despite the village's popularity with tourists, the locals remain grounded in their traditional customs and welcoming demeanor. You could easily spend an entire day exploring a myriad of authentic local businesses; for example, The Hawkshead Relish Company produces delicious chutneys, jams, and relishes crafted from locally sourced produce that you'll love.

Lastly, a visit to Hawkshead Brewery taproom is an experience in its own right, offering award-winning frothy ales and an unparalleled chance to mingle with the locals and enjoy authentic village life.

Luss

Nestled on the western shores of Loch Lomond in West Dunbartonshire, Scotland lies the charming village of Luss. As travelers make their way to this delightful destination, they are greeted with rows of picturesque cottages stretched alongside the water's edge. The village holds immense appeal for those who wish to experience the fascinating history, rich culture, and local lifestyle of Scotland.

The origins of Luss trace back to the early medieval period when it was a strategic location for crossing Loch Lomond. During the medieval times, Luss played a critical role, especially during the wars between Scotland and England. The village belonged to the Clan Colquhoun during the 16th century, and their family still owns the Luss Estate, preserving its heritage. In the 19th century, Luss attracted wealthy Victorians who built summer homes here. Today, the village remains an important conservation area designated in 1960, protecting its distinct character.

The Luss Parish Church and exquisite stained-glass windows are a prominent landmark in Luss. The Loch Lomond Shores is a must-visit destination for retail, leisure centers, and incredible restaurants. Visitors can also embark on several stunning hiking trails, affording breathtaking views of Loch Lomond, the Arrochar Alps, and Ben Lomond Mountain.

Luss is a village with a rich sense of community spirit, and its locals are proud of their heritage and traditions. The village hosts several events throughout the year, celebrating its history and culture, including the Luss Agricultural Show and the Luss Highland Gathering. These events showcase traditional Scottish music and dance, displaying the finest of local talents.

The natural surroundings of Luss remain unparalleled. Loch Lomond is the largest freshwater lake in the UK and is a hot spot for water activities such as boating, fishing, and swimming. Visitors can also enjoy the rolling hills and picturesque countryside that envelop the village, providing a tranquil atmosphere.

Luss attracts tourists worldwide, and its recent modern developments such as the Loch Lomond Shores complex and new accommodations cater to travelers' needs. Despite the transformations, Luss has stayed true to its core values, maintaining its charm and community spirit.

In conclusion, Luss is a must-visit destination and rightly deserves a place in the "100 Random Villages in the UK." With its combination of natural beauty, rich history, and thriving community, Luss is a unique gem waiting to be explored.

Megève

The charming village of Megève, nestled in the heart of the French Alps, has undergone a fascinating transformation over the centuries. While it was once an essential stopping point for pilgrims on their way to Rome during the Middle Ages, it was the vision of the Rothschild family in the early 20th century that truly put Megève on the map.

Baroness Noémie de Rothschild visited the village in the 1910s and was immediately struck by its beauty. She built the first ski resort in the region and soon Megève became the winter destination of choice for the rich and famous, including Winston Churchill and the Duke and Duchess of Windsor.

Despite its transformation into a luxurious ski resort, Megève has managed to hold onto its historical charm and character. Features such as the 14th-century Église Saint-Jean-Baptiste, medieval streets, and quaint fountains offer glimpses into the village's rich past.

However, there is more to Megève than just its history. It boasts a variety of cultural attractions, including the renowned Megève Jazz Festival featuring world-class musicians in an alpine setting, and the Megève Museum, with exhibits on the village's art and history.

But what truly sets Megève apart is its natural beauty. Surrounded by mountains and valleys, it provides a breathtaking backdrop for outdoor enthusiasts, with skiing and snowboarding available in the winter and hiking and biking in the summer. For those looking for a challenge, nearby Mont Blanc offers spectacular views for those brave enough to climb it.

Despite its fancy reputation, Megève has managed to maintain its local community and traditional way of life. Local businesses, like Les Glaçons de Megève, a renowned artisanal cheese producer, contribute to its unique character. Visitors can also experience the authentic alpine lifestyle by attending the weekly market and sampling the fresh produce and crafts sold by locals.

In conclusion, Megève is a perfect blend of history, culture, and natural beauty. Its evolution from a humble medieval village to a high-end ski resort has allowed it to maintain its legacy while accommodating the demands of modern travelers. Whether you're an outdoor enthusiast or a history buff, Megève is a must-visit destination for anyone seeking to experience France's illustrious past.

Nunney

The rolling hills of Somerset play host to one of the most delightful villages in the UK: Nunney. A bucolic environment where life moves at a slower pace, this charming town is as quintessential as they come. From the traditional village green to the inviting array of shops and pubs, every corner exudes the authentic tranquility of rural England.

But the heart of Nunney lies in its amazement-inspiring gem, Nunney Castle. Built in the 14th century by Sir John Delamare as a symbol of his family's wealth and power, it quickly became a cornerstone of the local community. Situated at the center of the village, Nunney Castle majestically towers above the surrounding greenery while mirrored in the dazzling stream down below, making for a truly picturesque sight.

Throughout history, the castle has served as a home to many influential individuals, including the Paulet family who once owned the land. They were heavily involved in the English Civil War, and today, the castle serves as a Grade I listed building and is home to an array of medieval fortifications that give one a glimpse into the past.

Aside from the castle, Nunney is also home to a handful of other noteworthy landmarks that are just as captivating. The All Saints Church is one such gem, dating all the way back to the 14th century, and is host to some of the finest stained glass windows in the country. Additionally, there is a quaint old mill formerly from the 1700s, which currently houses a charming café and an art gallery - just the spot for a lazy afternoon.

Visitors to Nunney can participate in the annual Nunney Street Market that attracts locals and visitors from all over the region. Here, they can sample an array of foods, crafts, and music that brings the quaint village streets to life.

Nature-lovers will rejoice when they visit Nunney. The gently flowing village stream and the green spaces that surround it offer the perfect escape from everyday life. Walking trails invite visitors to explore the rolling hills and take in the stunning countryside of Somerset.

Above all, Nunney boasts a tight-knit community who welcome visitors with open arms. The warm and friendly atmosphere that permeates the town is a testament to its enduring charm. Nunney is the perfect retreat for those who seek to escape the fast-paced modern world and immerse themselves in an authentic bygone era. One can easily see why it tops the list of the UK's most charming villages.

Portmeirion

Nestled on the Welsh coast, Portmeirion Village is a picturesque and unique gem that visitors cannot miss. Built between 1925 and 1975 by Sir Clough Williams-Ellis, a devoted advocate for the protection of the UK's natural beauty and historic architecture, Portmeirion combines Italianate architecture with artisanal elegance to create a village that celebrates the aesthetics of the Mediterranean while preserving the site's natural beauty.

Portmeirion boasts significant architecture that evokes wonder and creativity, such as the Gothic Watchtower, Bridge House, and The Dome. The Italian garden invites visitors to relax and take a break from the hustle and bustle of everyday life. The village is full of unique landmarks, such as the mock-Firenze tower, portraying the Tower of London's White Tower, and the main piazza that hosts the village's famous fête.

Portmeirion is a vibrant community that hosts a range of unique traditions and events, such as the Portmeirion Festival, where visitors can enjoy musicians and artists from around the world. The village also hosts weekly farmers' markets, which offer visitors the opportunity to indulge in local produce and artisanal products, providing visitors with a true taste of the area.

Surrounded by rolling hills and rugged coastlines, the stunning natural landscape surrounding Portmeirion adds to the village's appeal. Adventure enthusiasts will find themselves spoiled for choice, with hiking, mountain biking, and watersports being popular activities in the area.

Portmeirion has been featured in several films, documentaries, and TV series, such as the iconic 1960s TV series "The Prisoner." The village's shops, restaurants, and cafes serve local and unique cuisine, adding to the village's charm and appeal. Visitors can immerse themselves in the village's rich history by staying at one of the charming bed and breakfasts or hotels in Portmeirion.

Portmeirion Village is a whimsical and joyful testament to Sir Clough Williams-Ellis' vision for urbanism and history preservation. It encapsulates a true blend of culture, beauty, and excitement— an excellent destination for travelers seeking to explore the UK's history and cultural legacy.

Selworthy

Tucked away in the rolling hills of Somerset is the charming village of Selworthy. A hidden gem in the UK, this picturesque village is a favourite amongst those who long for a serene and scenic escape. The lush landscape and iconic thatched cottages make for an idyllic retreat, but Selworthy is so much more than just beautiful surroundings.

Dating all the way back to the medieval era, Selworthy has a rich history that is worth exploring. Its earliest recorded history dates back to the Domesday Book in 1086, and over the centuries, the village has witnessed many important events and developments that shaped its history. From the wool and cloth industry of the 16th century to the smugglers of the 18th and 19th centuries, Selworthy has a colourful past.

One of the most acclaimed landmarks in Selworthy is its church, which dates back to the 13th century. The stunning stone tower is an excellent example of English Gothic architecture, and the surrounding churchyard is a peaceful spot for contemplation. For those who love a good hike, Selworthy Beacon offers panoramic views of the surrounding area and is an ideal spot for nature enthusiasts.

But Selworthy is so much more than just landmarks; it boasts a vibrant community spirit that is felt throughout the village. From the annual Selworthy Fête, which brings the community together for a day of fun, music, games and food, to the local businesses like the Selworthy Pantry that sell home-made jams, chutneys and other treats using ingredients sourced from the village itself, Selworthy's charm is something to be experienced.

The natural surroundings of Selworthy only add to its allure. With miles of scenic hiking trails on Exmoor, grazing sheep and wild ponies dotting the rolling hills, and panoramic views of the Bristol Channel, Selworthy is a sight to behold.

In conclusion, Selworthy is more than just a picturesque village; it's a piece of living history. Its timeless charm and old-world elegance are perfect for contemporary travellers seeking the ideal blend of history, tradition and modern living in a world becoming increasingly complex. Selworthy serves as a reminder to the heritage and lifestyle of those who have lived there over the centuries, and it's a true haven of simplicity and natural beauty. So why not experience it for yourself and discover the timeless magic of Selworthy?

Turville

Nestled comfortably in the Chiltern Hills lies a dreamy, time-honored hamlet that has captured the hearts of visitors and film crews alike. Turville is a place where history, beauty, and charm converge in a perfect storm of idyllic bliss. Though it may be famous for it's on-screen appearances, this picturesque village offers so much more than meets the eye. Let's take a closer look at what makes Turville such a unique and special place to visit.

The story of Turville dates back to the Saxon era, when it consisted of two adjacent villages known as Turawille and Cobstone. Its rich history spans centuries and includes ownership by the monks of Notley Abbey and the notorious Hellfire Club founder, Sir Francis Dashwood's brother. Today, it's a thriving community with a population diverse in both background and age.

The village boasts an abundance of landmarks, but the 12th-century church of St. Mary the Virgin is a particular gem. This masterpiece of Norman architecture features an enchanting cemetery and is a beloved destination of visitors and locals alike. Other must-sees include the Old Rectory, a former home of The Vicar of Dibley, and the charming Cobstone Windmill that lords over the village from its chalk hilltop.

The community spirit here is palpable, and locals take pride in maintaining Turville's historic character while welcoming visitors and new businesses. The Turville Heath Cricket Club has been a staple of village life since the 1920s, and the annual Turville Heath Fete brings residents and visitors together for traditional country games, stalls, and refreshments.

Surrounded by the picturesque Chiltern Hills, Turville is a paradise for walkers and cyclists. The surrounding area is dotted with dense woodland trails, bridleways, and footpaths ripe for exploration. For history and nature lovers alike, Chiltern Open Air Museum offers a unique look into traditional building styles and rural living from bygone eras.

Turville may have made a name for itself on the screen but make no mistake, it's much more than a film set. This village exemplifies quintessential village life in the UK, with its rich history, cultural landmarks, natural beauty, and vibrant community. Come for a visit, and you might just find yourself never wanting to leave.

Warkworth

Nestled in the heart of Northumberland lies the charming village of Warkworth. This picturesque destination boasts a rich history, awe-inspiring natural landscapes, and a welcoming community that is sure to capture the hearts of its visitors. One of the most iconic features of Warkworth is its medieval castle, which stands tall over the village, a testament to the area's historic past.

Dating back to the 8th century, Warkworth's storied history is retraced in landmarks such as St. Lawrence's Church, a testament to the village's significance as a site for the early Christian church. During the middle ages, the Percy family, the Earls of Northumberland, used Warkworth as a strategic location, constructing the imposing Warkworth Castle, which remains a grand spectacle today.

Warkworth boasts a variety of landmarks that enthral visitors. Warkworth Castle is an imposing feature, drawing guests in with its picturesque location and grand facade. Visitors can explore its history through exhibits and guided tours. St. Lawrence's Church, a Gothic masterpiece, enthrals visitors with its intricate carvings and exquisite stained-glass windows. The secluded Warkworth Hermitage, a small chapel located in a river cave, adds an air of mystery and intrigue to visitors' experience.

The village's local traditions and community activities are captivating. Warkworth hosts the annual Warkworth Show, a must-visit event in August with its display of local produce, livestock, crafts as well as games and activities for all visitors. The village fosters a thriving arts scene, with local galleries and studios showcasing the work of local artists and craftspeople who proudly represent their village and its heritage. Whether you explore the village's unique local businesses like bakeries, galleries or boutiques, the true Warkworth spirit shines through.

Warkworth boasts stunning natural surroundings, set amidst the rolling hills and the picturesque River Coquet. Visitors can explore the local area on foot or by bike, with numerous trails and paths to suit all abilities. The surrounding countryside is also home to an array of wildlife such as red squirrels, otters, and various bird species, making it a nature enthusiast's paradise.

Warkworth's current village life highlights its community spirit. The lively and welcoming village ensures an array of events throughout the year, from open-air concerts to Christmas markets. You can explore pubs and restaurants, which offer local and international cuisine, to fully immerse yourself in the village living atmosphere.

West Wycombe

As you step foot into the charming village of West Wycombe, located in the heart of Buckinghamshire, it's hard not to feel like you've travelled back in time. This picturesque village is home to a variety of historic landmarks, unique traditions, and stunning natural surroundings, making it a perfect destination for those seeking to explore the history, culture, and natural beauty of the area.

West Wycombe's rich and varied history can be traced all the way back to the Roman era, but it was during the 18th century that the village flourished the most. This was thanks to Sir Francis Dashwood, the 11th Baron of Le Despencer, whose passions for Freemasonry, entertaining, politics and hedonism were instrumental in shaping the character of the village. Dashwood's eccentricity and philanthropy can be seen today in West Wycombe's many landmarks, cultural sites, and buildings, that he helped design and construct.

One of the most unique landmarks in West Wycombe is the Hellfire Caves, which were used as a secret meeting place for the notorious Hellfire Club, founded by Sir Francis Dashwood. These caves offer a unique glimpse into the extravagant and debauched lifestyle of the 18th century. Another stunning landmark is St. Lawrence Church, also known as the Golden Ball, which stands majestically on top of a hill overlooking the village and dates back to the 18th century.

Despite its rich history, the community of West Wycombe remains tightly-knit and proud of its heritage. Every year, they hold a traditional summer fete, celebrating the village's history and culture with music, food, and games. Local businesses, such as the Wycombe Brewery, which produces traditional English beers, contribute to the community's spirit which has managed to retain a link to its fascinating past.

West Wycombe's natural surroundings are as stunning as its history and culture. The village is surrounded by rolling hills, picturesque countryside, and farms, all of which make for some of the most beautiful walks in the area. One of the most popular walks is the Hellfire Caves Walk, which takes you on a beautiful stroll through the surrounding countryside surrounding West Wycombe.

Today, West Wycombe is both a thriving village with modern developments that reflect its past, and an important landmark in Buckinghamshire's rich history. It remains a perfect destination for anyone interested in travel, history, and cultural exploration. In conclusion, West Wycombe offers an unforgettable experience that showcases the unique character of the village, steeped in history.

Winchcombe

Nestled in the heart of the Cotswolds, Winchcombe is an idyllic village that exudes quintessential charm and boasts a rich history. Its most notable landmark is undoubtedly Sudeley Castle – once the home of King Henry VIII's final wife, Katherine Parr. Its impressive ruins and captivating exhibits within the castle's walls are an attraction in themselves, with visitors from across the globe eager to explore and soak in the historical beauty that exudes from this village.

History enthusiasts will be happy to know that Winchcombe's history dates back to the Saxon era when it was an important centre for wool production. In the Middle Ages, Winchcombe Abbey took centre stage as a pilgrimage site, attracting many visitors to the area. It became associated with the Tudor era through its association with the nearby Sudeley Castle, which played a crucial role in the period. Later, during the Civil War, the village became known for its support of the Parliamentarians, leading to its incorporation into the Commonwealth in 1646.

Hailes Abbey is another historical landmark located on the outskirts of Winchcombe. Founded in the 13th century, today its impressive ruins and the remains of its famed painted ceiling are a must-see for visitors.

Winchcombe's community spirit is as strong as ever, with a variety of events and activities taking place throughout the year. One of the most anticipated events is the annual Winchcombe Country Show, where visitors treat themselves to a range of exhibits, shows, and competitions. The village has a unique musical culture, hosting several music festivals throughout the year, including the Folk Festival and Jazz Festival.

Winchcombe is home to several unique local businesses, such as the Winchcombe Pottery, famous for its high-quality ceramics made using traditional techniques. You can also enjoy the area's rich history and local artistry by exploring the eclectic range of antique shops in the village.

Visitors can immerse themselves further in the natural surroundings and landscape features by venturing into the Cotswold Hills and the neighboring Cotswold Way – a long-distance walking trail that offers panoramic views of the area.

In conclusion, whether you're a history buff, adventurer, or just looking for a quintessential English village experience, Winchcombe is an ideal destination. Its blend of natural beauty, cultural sites, unique local businesses, and a thriving community spirit make it a place you'll not want to leave in a hurry.

Ashford-in-the-Water

Nestled in the heart of the Peak District National Park, Ashford-in-the-Water is a dreamy village that will transport you to a world of natural beauty, and a life that moves at a slower pace. Its history goes back over eight centuries, and you can see it in every nook and cranny of this charming place. The village is famous for its unique tradition of well dressing which dates back to the 14th century and is still celebrated with much enthusiasm.

The rural life in Ashford-in-the-Water is a must-see for anyone looking to discover the essence of English countryside. One of the most notable historical figures of the village was James Pinder, a local entrepreneur who built tunnels and roads for the transportation of limestone, thereby shaping the village we know today.

One of the most prominent features of Ashford-in-the-Water is the St. Michael and All Angels Church, which has stood ever since the 13th century. This church is an alluring spot for a serene moment or two, with magnificent stained glass windows, a Norman baptismal font, and ethereal chancel screen at hand. The Sheepwash Bridge, a 17th century bridge across the River Wye, is also a stunning sight that you will remember for years to come.

The village is home to several cultural sites, and none more so than its annual well-dressing festival, an incredible display of natural art at its finest. Over the third weekend in July, people come from all parts of England to witness these awe-inspiring creations made of flower petals, leaves, and seeds. The Lathkill Dale Nature Reserve and the Monsal Trail, perfect for those that love the outdoors and want to take a long walk, are also some of the best escapes from the city life.

Ashford-in-the-Water is also a cohesive community that is proud of its rich history and the serene streets that have remained unspoiled over the years. Visitors can immerse themselves in the everyday life of the village, have tea or a pint with the friendly locals, and stay at one of the cozy bed & breakfast places on the idyllic village streets.

In conclusion, Ashford-in-the-Water is the perfect antidote for anyone in search of a break from the hustle and bustle of city life. This wonderful village is an amalgamation of history, culture, and nature, all perfectly blended for the visitor's pleasure. So pack your bags, come to Ashford-in-the-Water, and witness the beauty that will steal your heart.

Beer

Looking for an authentic, off-the-beaten-path travel experience? Look no further than the charming village of Beer, nestled on the Jurassic Coast. This picturesque fishing village boasts a rich history, stunning landscapes, and a bustling harbor that has drawn visitors for centuries.

Beer's rich history stretches back to the Roman era and includes a prominent past as a port for trade, fishing, and smuggling. During the 18th and 19th centuries, the village prospered thanks to the booming fishing industry, which contributed significantly to the area's development. Beer was also an important wine and spirit producer due to its proximity to key markets. Notable historical figures such as Sir John Hayward, who established Beer as a health resort, and Captain Frederick Marryat, a famous British naval officer who lived in the area and wrote novels based on local stories, left a lasting impact on the village. During World War II, Beer played a crucial role in coastal defense, with many fishermen volunteering for service in the Royal Navy. Today, Beer remains a charming and historic village, with many reminders of its intriguing past.

In addition to its rich history, Beer's breathtaking landmarks, cultural sites, and geographical features make it a top destination for travelers. The beach is a key highlight of the village, surrounded by stunning cliffs that serve as a natural backdrop. Tourists can also visit fascinating cultural sites like Beer Quarry Caves, which date back to Roman times and were vital in the extraction of the local Beer stone.

Beer's charming architecture, thatched cottages, and winding streets create a unique atmosphere that's hard not to fall in love with. Local businesses provide a warm welcome to tourists, including quirky shops, art galleries, cafes, and seafood restaurants catering to all tastes. Beer Brewery, which offers locally brewed beer made from Devon malt and hops, is also worth a visit.

For those looking to explore the great outdoors, Beer provides an opportunity to discover the East Devon Area of Outstanding Natural Beauty, boasting stunning coastal cliffs, wildflowers, and green hills. The village is also the perfect base for exploring the nearby Jurassic Coast, which is home to rare geological wonders, winning beaches, and unique wildlife.

Lastly, Beer remains a thriving fishing village, and visitors can taste the local fresh catch from the fishing market. The village's strong sense of community and annual events, such as the Beer Regatta, Carnival Week, and the Beer R&B Festival, make it a must-visit destination for anyone seeking an authentic travel experience.

.

Clovelly

Nestled along the North Devon coast of England, the charming village of Clovelly is a traveler's dream come true. Its rich maritime history and cobbled streets beckon visitors who seek the quintessential English village experience.

Clovelly traces its roots back to the 9th century, when it was bequeathed to Saxon nobleman Aelfric. As the village grew into an epicenter of fishing commerce, merchants and traders from across Europe flocked to the area. The fishing industry prospered during the 16th and 17th centuries and played a significant role in the village's prominence.

Historical figures with ties to Clovelly include Charles Kingsley, who penned 'Westward Ho,' and John Rous, who financed its first school. Today, visitors can explore Clovelly's charming cobbled streets and bask in the beauty of its Court Gardens, while the Clovelly Fisherman's Museum offers a glimpse into the village's district maritime past.

The village's steep hill provides a stunning vantage point from where visitors can bask in the natural scenic beauty of the North Devon coast, where nearby walks and hikes offer endless opportunities for exploration. Clovelly's traditions and community events - such as the annual Lobster and Crab Feast - reflect the village's unique character and help visitors feel as though they have become one with its enchanting community.

Local businesses ranging from art galleries to cafes that serve up homemade delights contribute mightily to the village's charm. Today, Clovelly remains the proud hub of a thriving community, one that continues to entice visitors from far and wide with its impressive cobbled streets, breathtaking landmarks, and celebrations of long-standing traditions. It's easy to see why Clovelly has become a favorite location for movies and television shows alike.

In summary, Clovelly is an unmissable destination for travelers seeking out English charm, beauty, and history. Its fascinating streets, picturesque sites, and unique traditions culminate in a remarkable village experience that warrants a place on any wanderer's bucket list.

Cushendun

Nestled within the charming glens of County Antrim lies the captivating village of Cushendun. Its quaint setting and enchanting atmosphere embody the essence of Irish culture and heritage, making it a destination that travel enthusiasts should not miss.

Cushendun takes its name from the Irish words "Cois Abhann Duinne," which means "foot of the River Dun." Built in the 20th century as a model village for the estate workers of local landowner Ronald John McNeill, it has evolved into a thriving community with a rich history.

This picturesque village boasts marvelous scenery and unique architecture, including the stunning Tudor Revival-style Glenmona House that was once a hunting lodge. The lush gardens and lawns surrounding the mansion have become a favorite haunt for outdoor enthusiasts.

Another must-see attraction is the Cushendun Caves, a legendary spot that local folklore says was the birthplace of Cúchulainn, a mythic Irish warrior. The caves can only be entered during low tide, which gives visitors a thrilling adventure.

Cushendun is also renowned for preserving its rich heritage, steeped in old-world charm. One of its most celebrated traditions is the annual "May Day" celebrations, where the villagers gather for music, dancing, and a parade that marks the arrival of spring. The local residents take pride in sharing their heritage and inviting visitors to engage with their culture.

The village is an excellent base for exploring some of the most stunning natural scenery in Ireland, including the towering sea cliff at Torr Head that overlooks the vast Atlantic Ocean. Its proximity to breathtaking landscapes and rocky cliffs attracts both local and foreign visitors.

Cushendun takes pride in its strong community spirit, boasting a small population that welcomes visitors with open arms. It has several artisanal shops that sell locally made crafts, contributing to its vibrant community.

In summary, Cushendun is a cherished gem that showcases the best of Irish culture and hospitality. Its charming beauty, friendly people, and cultural heritage make it a must-see destination for all travelers planning a UK visit. Whether you're interested in a weekend getaway or considering moving to a new place, Cushendun should be at the top of your list.

Elterwater

Nestled in the heart of Cumbria's Lake District, Elterwater is a village that boasts picturesque landscapes, intriguing history and a lively community. A place where rural England's charm and beauty remain intact, this quaint village has something to offer to everyone who comes to visit.

With a past tightly intertwined with the slate industry of the region that goes all the way back to Roman times, Elterwater played a crucial role in the 18th and 19th centuries as a significant mining and quarrying hub, providing employment and a much-needed source of revenue.

Elterwater's cultural significance extends beyond the slate industry. Samuel Taylor Coleridge, the poet and friend of William Wordsworth, found inspiration in the rugged landscapes and natural beauty of the village and documented his stay in "Kubla Khan." The stone arch bridge, Elterwater Bridge, built in the 17th century, is a great example of Lakeland architecture. The St. John's Church with its Georgian-era build and traditional and contemporary architectural elements is another beautiful landmark worth visiting.

Elterwater's community spirit is alive and buzzing with artistic traditions and events. The village is a hub for artists and creatives, and the Elterwater Pottery is a testament to the traditional crafts and ceramics made by skilled craftsmen. The Elterwater Sheepdog Trials celebrate farming heritage and the breeding and training of sheepdogs, and the local community comes together to partake in this celebration every year.

Apart from the artistic and cultural heritage, Elterwater's natural surroundings are breathtaking. The Langdale Pikes' towering peaks dominate the skyline, offering stunning views over the countryside. Blea Tarn Nature Reserve is a protected area that attracts wildlife such as red deer, otters, golden eagles and ospreys, making Elterwater an excellent spot for nature lovers and outdoor enthusiasts.

With modern development in recent years, the village has an increased number of cafes, restaurants and accommodation options to cater to tourists and travellers. Whether one is interested in history, culture, nature or the outdoors, Elterwater is a destination that promises to delight and offer an authentic English rural experience.

Framlingham

Nestled in the heart of the beautiful county of Suffolk, East England, lies the idyllic village of Framlingham. A picture-perfect market town with a rich history dating back centuries, Framlingham has become a favorite destination for visitors from all over the world.

At the heart of the village lies the majestic Framlingham Castle. Built in the twelfth century by the powerful Earl of Norfolk, the castle has played a significant role in English history. Once a royal residence, it later became a tourist attraction, drawing visitors from far and wide.

But Framlingham offers so much more than just a castle. Its charming town center is strewn with cultural landmarks, such as the stunning medieval church of St. Michael and St. John. Visitors can marvel at the intricate stained glass windows and exquisite murals, depicting scenes from the Bible.

Beyond the cultural landmarks, Framlingham is a bubbling community with a strong sense of unity. There's something for everyone throughout the year, from the Framlingham Country Show, celebrating the village's farming heritage, to the Framlingham Soapbox Derby, where homemade carts race down the town's steep hill.

And it's not just community activities that delight visitors. Framlingham has an impressive variety of independent businesses, such as the renowned Earl Soham Brewery, which produces some of the finest craft beers in the region, and the Organic Farm Shop, with its local produce of exceptional quality.

Nature-lovers are in for a treat as Framlingham is surrounded by lush hills and leafy greenery. Not far away is the exquisite seaside town of Aldeburgh, known for its shingle beaches, stunning views, and picturesque seafood restaurants.

Framlingham is a place where tradition meets modern living. Visitors can enjoy the ancient, time-honored customs passed down through generations, whilst benefiting from the convenience of a modern-day village. It is a truly unforgettable experience, and one that visitors will cherish for years to come.

Godshill

Godshill, a charming village on the Isle of Wight, is a perfect destination for anyone looking for a slice of British history and culture. The village boasts a rich past reaching as far back as the Domesday Book of 1086 and was a hub for wool production during the medieval period. The village was also a popular pilgrimage site, with All Saints' Church, built in the 14th century, attracting visitors from far and wide to admire the incredible wall paintings and stained-glass windows.

Godshill is famous for its enchanting thatched cottages and a one-fifteenth-scale model village that showcases the unique architecture of the village. The model village is a popular attraction and is adored for the intricate details of its model houses, gardens, and streets. Visitors can take a leisurely stroll around the miniature village, marvelling at its picturesque thatched roofs and charming streets.

Apart from the model village, All Saints' Church is another gem in Godshill's crown. The church stands atop a hill overlooking the village, and its gothic-style adds to the charm of the village. The magnificent murals and stained-glass windows that cover the walls are a testament to the church's rich history.

Nature lovers will delight in Godshill's picturesque countryside. The village's footpaths and woodland trails offer a leisurely walk where visitors can stop and smell the roses. The rolling hills and natural surroundings make it an idyllic destination, perfect for those seeking tranquillity.

Godshill's unique charm is further accentuated by its community activities, which give visitors an insight into the village's vibrant cultural scene. The annual Godshill May Fair is one such event that visitors shouldn't miss. The fair, with its carnival atmosphere, locally-made crafts, and live music, is a fitting showcase for the village's unique community spirit.

Exploring the village's local businesses is also an exciting experience. From vintage tea rooms to gift shops that stock locally-made crafts, visitors can put together a bespoke collection of products that will remind them of their trip to Godshill.

Godshill is an enchanting village with a timeless appeal. Its charm, natural beauty, and rich history make it a destination that should be on everyone's list of places to visit. Visitors can expect an unforgettable experience in this idyllic village.

Hutton-le-Hole

Nestled amongst the rolling hills and stunning scenery of the North York Moors National Park lies the picturesque village of Hutton-le-Hole. This hidden gem is renowned for its idyllic stream and the Ryedale Folk Museum, offering visitors the perfect blend of history, culture, and stunning natural surrounds.

Dating back to the 12th century, Hutton-le-Hole has a rich and fascinating history, having once been part of the vast estates of the Earls of Rutland. From surviving the infamous Black Death of the 14th century to being the home of the Hey family, Lords of the Manor for over 300 years, this village has seen its fair share of remarkable events and figures.

Visitors can explore the area's rich heritage and culture through the Ryedale Folk Museum, which houses a vast collection of historic artifacts from prehistoric times right through to the Victorian era. The picturesque stream also offers a perfect spot for a leisurely stroll, while the annual duck race draws communities together in good-natured fun and festivities.

However, what truly sets Hutton-le-Hole apart is its unique sense of community and well-preserved traditions. The village's annual scarecrow festival is a sight to behold, with handmade scarecrows of all shapes and sizes displayed throughout the village, attracting visitors from far and wide.

Beyond its charming street scenes and historic buildings, visitors can also discover adventure in the North York Moors National Park. Surrounded by breathtaking landscapes, Hutton-le-Hole is a perfect base for both hikers and cyclists. Plus, birdwatchers will delight in the rare bird species found in the area.

Last but not least, Hutton-le-Hole has a vibrant and welcoming community that takes pride in preserving the village's unique character. Local businesses like the artisan coffee shop, woolen mill, and stone carving workshop have become community anchors, while annual fairs and festivals like the Christmas market and summer fair keep the community spirit alive and thriving.

In conclusion, Hutton-le-Hole is a charming and memorable village that has something for everyone. Whether you're a history buff, culture enthusiast, or nature lover, this village will satisfy your cravings. So, why not come and explore Hutton-le-Hole for yourself? You'll be sure to leave feeling enchanted and inspired.

Lacock

The charming village of Lacock, located in Wiltshire, is steeped in a rich history that spans back to the 13th century. Founded by the influential Ela of Salisbury, the village and Abbey have seen many changes over the years, transforming from a religious institution to a family home, and finally, a National Trust property. Today, Lacock's medieval streets and impressive Abbey remain incredibly well-preserved, attracting visitors from all over the world.

One of the standout features of Lacock are its streets that seem to have been frozen in time. The village is a living museum and one can almost see the shadows of past residents strolling through the narrow, cobbled lanes, which remain largely untouched by the passage of time. The beautiful Abbey, with its stunning architecture and manicured gardens, is a must-visit landmark while in the village. This iconic monument has featured in several movies and television shows, including Harry Potter and Downton Abbey.

Another important historical site in Lacock is St. Cyriac's Church, which dates back to the 15th century. The church is renowned for its magnificent stained glass windows and stunning Elizabethan tombs of the Sharington family. Additionally, Lacock boasts a 14th-century tithe barn that is now a community center, once used for storing grain and cloth.

Lacock is a tight-knit community with a strong sense of pride in its heritage. The village holds various events throughout the year, including the highly popular Lacock at Christmas festival. The streets are festooned with twinkling lights and lively festivities, brimming with jubilant Christmas spirit. The annual scarecrow trail is another firm favorite with locals, who create and display their unique scarecrows.

The picturesque countryside surrounding Lacock offers visitors an opportunity to explore idyllic landscapes, charming cottages, and flowing rivers. Relaxing boat trips or leisurely riverside strolls along the River Avon are popular pastimes. Remarkably, Lacock's popularity as a tourist destination hasn't changed its character and charming village feel. While attracting visitors from all corners of the globe, the village remains true to its roots and tradition, welcoming those who appreciate its natural surroundings and rich heritage.

In summary, Lacock is an enchanting village offering a unique blend of historical landmarks, cultural attractions, and natural beauty. With well-preserved medieval streets and Abbey, combined with a strong community spirit and idyllic countryside surroundings, Lacock is an unforgettable destination for history buffs, culture lovers, and nature enthusiasts.

Mousehole

As you drive along the Cornish coast, you'll come across a charming little village called Mousehole. This quaint fishing village boasts of a fascinating history, rich culture, stunning natural surroundings, and a vibrant community that's sure to leave a lasting impression on visitors. The village's history dates back to the 13th century, and since then, it has been a prominent hub for the Cornish coast. The village's economy thrived on tin and copper smuggling activities during the 17th and 18th century, and it was home to some of the notorious smugglers of the time.

Mousehole is known for its iconic landmarks like the Mousehole Harbour, the village church, and the tiny harbor beach. The harbor is the heart of the village, and the perfect spot to watch the sunset. The village's Museum of Legends and Folklore provides a captivating glimpse into the area's rich history, traditions, and legends. You'll be fascinated by the quirky tales and legends that surround Mousehole.

One of the most unique traditions in Mousehole is the famous Christmas lights display. The entire village is bedecked with thousands of twinkling lights, creating a magical atmosphere that's truly a sight to behold. The annual display attracts thousands of visitors, and it stretches along the harbor, quayside, and up into the village. Another treasured tradition is the annual Tom Bawcock's Eve, which is celebrated with a lantern procession, traditional Cornish music, and storytelling.

Mousehole's natural surroundings and landscape features are equally awe-inspiring. The village is situated between two granite headlands, offering a stunning view over Mounts Bay. The coastline around Mousehole is a renowned destination for surfing, swimming, and fishing. The nearby St. Michael's Mount is another natural landmark and a must-visit destination for visitors to Mousehole. The island is home to a medieval fortress, a castle, and beautiful gardens.

Today, Mousehole is a vibrant village that retains its traditional Cornish charm. The village comes alive during several festivals throughout the year, showcasing the community spirit and pride in their heritage. The village's unique character is further enhanced by its artisan shops, bakeries, and art galleries.

In conclusion, a visit to Mousehole is an absolute must for anyone seeking an authentic Cornish experience. This charming village offers a perfect blend of history, culture, natural beauty, and modern-day amenities. Whether you're exploring the rich history and traditions or soaking in the stunning landscape, Mousehole has something for everyone.

Polperro

Polperro: A Captivating Coastal Village Brimming with History and Charm Nestled along the stunning Cornish coastline lies the picturesque village of Polperro, oozing with character and allure. The village boasts a rich cultural heritage, dating back to the Bronze Age era. Visitors can wander through the winding streets of white-washed cottages, ancient churches, and Gothic houses, immersing themselves in the village's history. Polperro's unique character stems from its fishing and smuggling past, which continues to captivate tourists from across the globe.

Polperro's origins can be traced back centuries when our ancestors mined tin and copper in the surrounding hills. During the medieval era, it was bustling as a hub for trading, shipping, and fishing, with a busy harbor that brought in many vessels. However, in the 18th and 19th centuries, smuggling became a lucrative business that fueled the village's growth. The village's notorious smugglers and secret tunnels are still a source of intrigue today.

One of the most notable figures in Polperro's history was Zephaniah Job, a local farmer and fisherman who became a prominent smuggler and leader of one of the most notorious gangs. He managed to evade the excise officers for years, but his luck eventually ran out, and he was caught and hanged in 1831. His daring exploits have since become a legend, adding to the village's fascination.

Visitors can explore many iconic landmarks and features in Polperro, such as the bustling harbor and the Polperro Heritage Museum, which immerses visitors in the village's seafaring and smuggling history. The winding streets and alleyways are a joy to behold, with ancient churches, Gothic houses, and whitewashed cottages that epitomize the village's unique heritage.

Polperro's vibrant and proud community keeps its heritage alive through its traditions and activities. The Polperro Festival is a highlight of the year, with locals dressing up in traditional costumes, holding craft fairs, live music events, and a colorful parade through the streets. The Fishermen's Choir is another unique and charming aspect of village life. Visitors can also explore the local businesses, such as the Kings Arms pub, dating back to the 15th century, the Shell House Gallery, offering stunning seashell art and jewelry, and the Polperro Bakery, tempting visitors with fresh, delicious baked goods.

Polperro's stunning natural surroundings are the icing on the cake. The rolling hills, rugged cliffs, and stunning views over the sea, combined with charming hamlets and historic landmarks, make exploring the countryside a joy. The Talland Bay Beach is a beautiful spot for swimming, surfing, or sunbathing, while visitors can also enjoy dolphin watching in the surrounding waters.

Rye

Discovering Rye: A Glimpse into England's Rich Heritage and Culture
Rye, a village located in the tranquil southeastern corner of England, is a hidden gem that offers a unique insight into the country's rich history and culture. This piece explores Rye's well-preserved medieval architecture and literary connections, the village's tight-knit community, and its natural surroundings.

Rye's history stretches back to medieval England when it served as a crucial trading port in the 13th century. The village played a fundamental role during the Hundred Years' War between England and France in the 14th century, where it became a significant hub for prominent figures such as Henry VIII, Queen Elizabeth I, and Charles I. Today, Rye's historic buildings and structures capture its unique history and are treasured.

The village's well-preserved medieval architecture is an exceptional aspect of Rye. Narrow cobbled streets, ancient pub fronts over timber-framed buildings, and notable landmarks such as St. Mary's Church and Ypres Tower add to the town's charm. St. Mary's Church boasts impressive stained glass windows and beautiful architecture, while Ypres Tower, a 14th-century fortification, offers a glimpse into Rye's intriguing past as a center for wool trade.

Rye's literary history is another significant attraction. Celebrated writers like Henry James, E. F. Benson, and Radclyffe Hall called the village home and wrote about their experiences. Visitors can take a literary trail through various locations in the town that inspired these talented writers.

Rye's community is tight-knit and treasures their village's traditions and customs. The annual Bonfire Night celebrations that take place on November 5th is a significant event for the villagers. The event features a lively parade and a towering bonfire that lights up the night sky, recounting Guy Fawkes' failed attempt to blow up parliament in 1605. Rye is also home to local businesses such as Rye Pottery, which has been operating for over 200 years, producing unique handcrafted ceramics.

Rye's natural surroundings are breathtaking, with rolling hills that are part of the nearby High Weald Area of Outstanding Natural Beauty, offering visitors beautiful countryside and several nature reserves. Additionally, the village is in close proximity to the coast with golden sand beaches, stunning sea views, and dramatic cliffs that allure outdoor enthusiasts.

Rye has embraced modernization while preserving its traditional and historical engagements. The village has a thriving artistic self-contained with numerous cultural events and festivals happening throughout the year.

Shaftesbury

Nestled among the rolling hills of the Dorset countryside lies the idyllic village of Shaftesbury. Its most iconic landmark is the picturesque Gold Hill, which has captured the hearts of many due to its charming cobblestone streets and honey-hued buildings. With its fame and recognition, it has become a popular location for media and advertising.

Shaftesbury played a significant role in medieval times as a center of commerce with a bustling market attracting merchants and traders from far and wide. This village was also graced with notable historical figures, including King Alfred the Great and the philosopher and mathematician Thomas Hobbes, famous for his seminal work, Leviathan, which explored the nature of government and society.

One of the village's most outstanding landmarks is the 14th-century Abbey Church of St. Mary, with its intricate stained glass windows and Gothic architecture. Shaftesbury boasts many cultural offerings, including the Shaftesbury Arts Centre, a community-driven organization that hosts a vibrant program of theatre, music, and visual arts events.

The Gold Hill continues to be the pride of Shaftesbury, featuring in many television shows and movies. The Hovis bread commercial, showcasing a young boy cycling down the steep slope carrying a loaf of bread, is still an iconic image of the village. Visitors from different parts of the world come to see this captivating hill.

Shaftesbury is also renowned for its unique traditions and community activities that contribute to its charm. The Shaftesbury Carnival is a colorful procession of floats and costumes that takes place annually. The Shaftesbury Fringe Festival also celebrates the arts in all their forms.

If you're looking for a place to relax and rejuvenate, Shaftesbury's picturesque landscape, vibrant forests, and rolling fields provide the perfect backdrop for hiking and nature walks. The Cranborne Chase and West Wiltshire Downs Area of Outstanding Natural Beauty is a nearby attraction that offers many recreational activities.

Overall, Shaftesbury captures the essence of rural charm and beauty with its rich history, cultural offerings, and stunning natural surroundings. Whether you are interested in history, culture, or simply want to immerse yourself in the breathtaking scenery of the Dorset countryside, Shaftesbury should undoubtedly be at the top of your list.

Tobermory

Nestled among the rolling hills of Scotland's Isle of Mull, the colorful village of Tobermory has earned fame as the setting for beloved children's show "Balamory". But beyond its vibrant waterfront facades lies a fascinating destination with a rich history and unique traditions to match any traveler's interests.

It all began in the late 18th century when the village was founded as a fishing haven. Over time, Tobermory grew in importance as a central port and key player in Scotland's whisky trade - exporting from local distilleries through the harbor. Today, visitors can explore the village's historic past by way of important figures such as Lachlan Macquarie, a local hero who later became the governor of New South Wales and Alexander McLean, a 19th-century shipbuilder pivotal in the establishment of Tobermory's port.

The village boasts a range of landmarks and cultural sites, but none quite as iconic as the vibrant colors of the old sea-facing buildings. Originally painted in subtle pastels, these structures received a new coat of brilliant hues in the 1980s as part of a tourism initiative. Other must-see features of Tobermory include the Mull Museum and Mull Theatre, both showcasing the history and culture of the region.

But what makes Tobermory truly special is its strong sense of community and the unique local businesses and traditions that thrive throughout the village. Visitors can experience the annual Christmas craft fair, hosted by An Tobar Arts Centre, or make their way to the annual Mull Highland Games, celebrating traditional Scottish sports and customs. And it's hard not to take note of Maclean's Bakery, a staple since the 1920s, where traditional recipes have been the key to delicious baked goods for generations.

Tobermory's natural surroundings complete the idyllic picture. From the stunning Ardnamurchan Peninsula to the Isle of Iona, there is breathtaking beauty around every corner. The natural harbor is a sight to behold, as is the local wildlife that call the nearby hills and forests home. Red deer and eagles are among the many creatures to be spotted while hiking, kayaking, or simply exploring the great outdoors.

Despite its small size, Tobermory is a lively village that caters to the needs of residents and visitors alike. The village's thriving arts scene, eco-tourism, and culinary offerings set the stage for a warm and welcoming stay. Whether you're a history buff or a lover of culture, nature, or delicious baked goods, Tobermory has something to fascinate and inspire you.

Walberswick

If you're looking for a picturesque coastal village that's rich in history, art, and culture, then Walberswick is a must-visit destination. Nestled on the Suffolk coast, this charming village boasts a rustic charm that draws visitors from all over.

Walberswick has a fascinating history that dates back to the 11th century. As an important fishing village, it was a crucial transportation hub and a popular spot for trade and commerce. Later, in the 19th century, Walberswick's breathtaking landscapes and inspiring scenery attracted artists and writers such as Charles Rennie Mackintosh and Philip Wilson Steer.

As you explore the village, you'll come across several key landmarks and cultural sites. The Church of St. Andrew is undoubtedly the most famous, with its stunning Gothic architecture and breathtaking stained-glass windows. And don't miss the old ferry crossing, which has been in use since medieval times.

If you're an art lover, you'll be delighted with the vibrant art scene in Walberswick. There are plenty of galleries and studios showcasing some of the UK's top talent. And you won't want to miss the famous Annual Crabbing competition, which draws locals and tourists alike for a day of fun and crustacean-themed activities.

Walberswick's natural surroundings are truly stunning. With its sandy beach and rugged dunes, the coastal landscape takes your breath away. Venture inland, and you'll discover a world of heathlands, riverbanks, and shaded woods, perfect for long walks or adventurous bike rides.

Despite being a popular tourist destination, Walberswick has a strong sense of community spirit. Throughout the year, there are plenty of events and activities that bring people together, from live music performances to Easter bonnet parades. And with interesting local businesses, such as gourmet restaurants and quirky independent shops, there's always something new to explore.

Whether you're looking for a place to visit or a place to call home, Walberswick offers something for everyone. With its charming atmosphere, friendly locals, and lively community spirit, it's easy to see why this village has become one of the UK's most beloved destinations.

Boscastle

Nestled on the picturesque north coast of Cornwall, Boscastle is one of the UK's hidden gems. With its rich fishing history, notorious smuggling trade and dramatic coastline, this rural village is a perfect destination for any traveler seeking to learn more about the country's unique culture and history.

Boscastle has a rich history dating back to the 12th century when it was recognized as a small fishing village. It grew into a prosperous port town, attracting traders, settlers and travelers from all over the world. But it was the advent of the smuggling trade in the 18th century that really put Boscastle on the map, with battles between smugglers and authorities becoming commonplace.

Several landmarks define the village, including the picturesque harbor, surrounded by steep cliffs, rolling hills and bobbing fishing boats. The coastline is another popular attraction, with rock formations, hidden coves and sandy beaches. The Museum of Witchcraft and Magic and nearby Tintagel castle offer spellbinding insights into the village's unique culture and history.

One of the most unique events in Boscastle is the annual 'Washing of the Fishing Boats', a ceremony in which local fishermen wash their boats and equipment in the harbor. The village is home to several local businesses, including a pottery shop, a national trust watermill and several family-run cafes and restaurants known for their delicious seafood dishes.

Boscastle's rugged coast, steep cliffs and rolling hills make it an ideal destination for walkers and outdoor enthusiasts. The village lies on the South West Coast Path, a 630-mile walking route passing through some of the UK's most stunning coastal landscapes. Boscastle's strong community spirit is one of its most compelling features, with a thriving arts scene and regular community events.

Boscastle is a unique and fascinating destination that offers a glimpse into Cornwall's rich history and unique culture. With its stunning natural surroundings, charming village life, and fascinating landmarks and traditions, it's a must-visit for any traveler seeking an authentic taste of rural UK life.

Bourton-on-the-Water

As you wander through the Cotswold Area of Outstanding Natural Beauty, you'll discover the charming village of Bourton-on-the-Water. This inviting English village has a rich history stretching back to medieval times and is renowned for its picturesque beauty. Its distinctive tone and texture come from the Cotswold stone that many of the buildings in the village are constructed from, extracted from surrounding hills. The village developed as a center for farming, quarrying, and milling, and soon became significant in the wool trade in England.

The River Windrush winds through the village, and small stone bridges are dotted throughout, giving it the nickname "the Venice of the Cotswolds." The Bourton-on-the-Water Model Village is a famous landmark and offers visitors a unique perspective on this charming destination. The Fosse Gallery is another notable attraction that showcases the artistic talent in the village.

Bourton-on-the-Water is a village that takes pride in its traditions and community spirit. Visitors can enjoy hitting the shops, cafes, and pubs that support the local way of life. You must experience Mrs. Moo's café and taste their delicious cream teas along with ice cream. Or grab a bite to eat from the Lamb Inn that serves hearty meals.

If you're looking to escape the city's hustle and bustle, Bourton-on-the-Water is the perfect place. Families and retirees often visit this vibrant village. The annual Bourton-on-the-Water Football in the River is a highlight that sees two teams play in the shallow waters of the river and is a charity event. There is plenty to explore, from the rolling hills and verdant fields that surround the village to bird-watching at the RSPB's reserve. Nearby attractions also include the Chedworth Roman Villa, a well-preserved Roman villa complex, and the Cotswold Wildlife Park.

Bourton-on-the-Water is a special place that continues to captivate visitors and locals alike. It is a quintessential English village where the community cherishes its traditions. The village's rich heritage, natural beauty, and vibrant way of life are an invitation to enjoy a slower pace of life and appreciate what this charming destination has to offer.

Broadway

As you wander through the winding streets of Broadway, it's hard not to feel transported to a simpler time. The charming village in the Cotswold region exudes a timeless beauty that has attracted visitors for centuries. But it's not just the picture-perfect scenery that draws people to Broadway; it's also the vibrant arts scene and strong sense of community that make it a truly special destination.

Broadway's history stretches back to Roman times, but it was during the 16th century that the village truly flourished as a hub for weaving and wool production. However, it was the 19th century that marked a turning point, as Broadway became a haven for artists such as J.M.W. Turner and William Morris. The beauty of the village captured their imaginations, and their legacy lives on to this day. The annual Broadway Arts Festival celebrates the area's rich artistic heritage, while local artisans and independent shops keep traditions alive.

Broadway's natural surroundings are no less inspiring, with rolling hills, tranquil streams, and an abundance of wildlife. There are plenty of opportunities for hiking and exploring the picturesque countryside. And while Broadway may be steeped in history, it's also a thriving modern village with a bustling farmers' market and an array of tempting restaurants and cafes.

It's hard not to fall under the spell of Broadway's enchanting atmosphere. The historic St. Eadburgha Church and the centuries-old coaching inn, The Lygon Arms, are just two of the village's many landmarks. And then there's Broadway Tower, which offers stunning panoramic views of the surrounding countryside.

But perhaps most special of all is the sense of community that pervades Broadway. Locals still keep alive the ancient tradition of Morris dancing, and the village's residents take great pride in their traditions and heritage. This is a place where you can escape the hustle and bustle of modern life and reconnect with something deeper and more meaningful.

Broadway is undoubtedly one of the 100 most random and enchanting villages in the UK. Its quintessential beauty, rich history, lively arts scene, and deep-rooted sense of community make it a destination that's not to be missed. So why not wander the winding streets of Broadway for yourself and experience all that this magical village has to offer?

Castleton

Nestled amidst the rolling hills of the Peak District, Castleton is a charming village that is bathed in authenticity and steeped in history. The picturesque setting and outstanding natural beauty of the area make it a must-visit destination for those looking to experience the best that the British countryside has to offer.

Castleton's compelling history is reflected in the village's industrial past, with the legacy of the once-thriving lead-mining industry still visible today. During the Tudor era, the village earned a royal charter, cementing its status as a hub of trade and commerce. Sir Richard Arkwright, one of the key figures of the Industrial Revolution, hailed from Castleton, further cementing its place in history.

At the heart of the village lies one of its most iconic landmarks, Mam Tor, fondly referred as the "Shivering Mountain." This imposing peak has played a significant role in the history of the village, providing a natural defensive fortification during times of conflict. The Devil's Arse caverns, found at the foot of Mam Tor, are also a significant geological feature of the area.

Castleton boasts a rich cultural heritage embodied by structures such as the Norman-style St Edmund's Church that dates back to the 12th century, renowned for its stunning stained-glass windows. The village is also a hub of artistic expression, with numerous galleries showcasing the vibrant works of local artists.

One of the most notable events in Castleton's social calendar is the annual Garland Ceremony, a colorful celebration held every May. The festivities consist of local children parading through the streets with garlands on their heads, accompanied by traditional music and dance. Outdoor enthusiasts will appreciate the village's scenic trails, perfect for hiking, cycling, and rock climbing.

The breathtaking natural landscapes surrounding Castleton are a significant draw for visitors. The towering limestone cliffs and crags provide a dramatic backdrop for hikers and climbers, and the Mam Tor area is particularly popular. The Blue John Caverns, a wonder of nature located nearby, is a breathtaking sight, with intricately lit chambers and magnificent stalactites and stalagmites.

Castleton is a thriving community that exudes a strong sense of tradition and maintains an impressive tourism industry. For those seeking an authentic British village experience, it is the perfect destination, providing a window into the rich history, timeless culture, and stunning natural beauty of the Peak District.

Corbridge

Nestled in the heart of Northumberland, England, lies the charming village of Corbridge, a must-see destination for history buffs and nature lovers alike. With its rich Roman heritage intertwined with traditional village charm, Corbridge boasts a unique and captivating appeal to both visitors and residents. Its unique character has earned it a place in the book "100 Random Villages in the UK", highlighting the many fascinating aspects that make it an exciting place to explore.

Corbridge boasts an illustrious Roman past that dates back to the invasions of Roman Britain. A significant military supply base was stationed here to support the Empire's military campaigns, leaving a lasting legacy that can still be seen today. The Roman Town of Corbridge, built around AD 140, stands as a testament to the impressive workmanship of the period. Visitors can explore the ancient town's many preserved Roman artifacts, including a Roman floor mosaic that once adorned a high-status Roman house.

Aside from the Roman Town, Corbridge boasts many other key landmarks, including St. Andrew's Church, a 13th-century place of worship known for its unique stained glass windows and fascinating historical artifacts. Corbridge Bridge, situated on the River Tyne, is also a record-worth site that attracts visitors every year.

Corbridge's thriving community cherishes the town's traditions while welcoming newcomers and visitors with open arms. One of its annual events, the Corbridge Festival, is a popular local arts and music festival that draws performers from far and wide.

Those seeking to enjoy the great outdoors won't be disappointed by Corbridge's breathtaking natural surroundings. With rolling hills, beautiful countryside, and numerous walking trails that reveal some of the most stunning landscapes in the region, visitors will be spoiled for choice. Nearby Hadrian's Wall, a symbol of the Roman Empire's northern frontier, offers unforgettable scenic views along its winding historical path.

Lastly, residents of Corbridge enjoy the benefit of a thriving community spirit, with a relatively low crime rate and a robust property market featuring a wide range of attractive homes for sale or rent, catering to different budgets.

In conclusion, Corbridge's unique blend of Roman history, traditional charm, community spirit, and captivating natural beauty make it an unforgettable destination for anyone seeking to explore the rich tapestry of Northumberland's cultural heritage.

Alfriston

Alfriston is a charming village nestled in the heart of the South Downs National Park in East Sussex, UK. Its picturesque thatched cottages, winding streets, and ancient churches make it a haven for history buffs and nature lovers alike.

But Alfriston's real claim to fame is its central role in the Arts and Crafts movement of the late 19th and early 20th centuries. The village's historic Clergy House, owned and managed by the National Trust, takes visitors on a journey back in time. It was here, in this 14th-century building, that the Arts and Crafts movement was born. The house's beautiful interiors, with their handcrafted furniture and exquisite decoration, have captivated many artists and designers over the years, including William Morris himself.

Alfriston's history dates back to the 14th century, when its most famous landmark, St. Andrew's Church, was constructed. The church's stunning mix of architectural styles, including Norman, Gothic, and 14th-century Decorated styles, continues to impress visitors to this day.

The village's rich history is also reflected in its annual Alfriston Festival, a celebration of the arts and culture of the area. The festival is a popular event, attracting visitors from far and wide with its classical music performances, art exhibitions, and literary talks.

Alfriston's independent shops and cafes are another draw for visitors, with homemade cakes and unique crafts made by local artisans on offer. The village's natural surroundings are also a feast for the senses, with the River Cuckmere meandering through the nearby countryside and the Seven Sisters Country Park offering stunning cliff walks and panoramic views of the English Channel.

Despite its rich history, Alfriston is not frozen in time. Its thriving community and modern amenities make it a popular destination for travelers of all ages. The village's Clergy House offers a unique glimpse into the past and a chance to learn more about the Arts and Crafts movement that once characterized the area.

Avebury

Avebury is more than a mere village. It is a treasure trove of the United Kingdom's history and natural wonders that will leave you awestruck. Nestled in the heart of Wiltshire, Avebury lets you travel back in time while enjoying the picturesque countryside scenery that surrounds it.

The Stone Circle at Avebury, which dates back to the Neolithic period over 4,500 years ago, is shrouded in mystery. It is a religious and gathering site for the local community, made from several stones that weigh up to 40 tons, and were transported from distant sites with great precision. Over time, Avebury grew around the stone circle as commerce and trade thrived. The area was visited by notable historical figures, including King Alfred the Great.

The village boasts several other significant landmarks for history enthusiasts, including the West Kennet Long Barrow, which is an ancient burial site that illuminates the ancient ritual practices of the area. The Avebury Manor and Garden, dating back to the 16th century, presents an opportunity to walk through historical moments and witness the beauty of the gardens.

Not only is Avebury rich in history, but its community also boasts several unique cultural practices. The monthly farmers' markets showcase locally-produced goods, while the bi-annual street fair celebrates the crafts, music, and food of the community. The annual Morris dance competition, "Avebury Hengehop," unites the country's celebrated Morris dance traditions.

The natural surroundings of Avebury provide a remarkable experience for hikers and cyclists. The North Wessex Downs Area of Outstanding Natural Beauty embraces the breathtaking landscapes of rolling hills, wildflowers and stunning vistas. There are endless trails for outdoor enthusiasts to explore.

Avebury's charm is not lost on the locals. The village boasts not only a range of businesses but also a close-knit community that brings their warmth and welcoming spirit to the many festivals, fairs, and events throughout the year. Be sure to enjoy the workshops and events hosted by local artisans and craftspeople.

In conclusion, Avebury is an unforgettable village that is a must-visit for those desiring to experience the UK's history and natural beauty. It is a community that is proud of its heritage while continuously providing moments of warmth and comfort through its unique cultural practices. Avebury is truly a wonder.

Betws-y-Coed

Nestled amongst the rugged peaks of Snowdonia National Park lies the charming village of Betws-y-Coed. This idyllic haven is a gateway to one of the UK's most breathtaking natural wonders, offering visitors the chance to immerse themselves in the rich cultural heritage of the local community.

Betws-y-Coed has a remarkable history, dating back to the early 14th century when it served as a small religious retreat. In the late 19th century, the arrival of the railway cemented its status as a popular tourist destination, attracting visitors from far and wide to explore the awe-inspiring natural beauty of Snowdonia.

One of the most notable landmarks in Betws-y-Coed is the ancient church of St. Michael, which stands proudly as a testament to the village's past. The bridge over the River Conwy provides a stunning focal point for the area, offering breathtaking views of the surrounding countryside. Artisan shops and galleries are also scattered throughout the village, showcasing unique crafts and artwork created by local artists.

Betws-y-Coed has a bustling community spirit, with a range of local events and activities throughout the year. The Snowdonia Marathon, one of the UK's most challenging long-distance races, takes place here, as well as the annual Betws-y-Coed Agricultural Show, which celebrates the best of the local farming community. The Lyric theatre also hosts live music, dramas, and other performances throughout the year.

The natural surroundings of Betws-y-Coed are a major draw for visitors. Offering sweeping views of the Snowdonia mountains and the River Conwy, guests can take part in a range of outdoor activities, such as hiking, kayaking, and rock climbing. Wildlife enthusiasts may be lucky enough to spot red squirrels, otters, and peregrine falcons wandering through the nearby Snowdonia National Park.

Today, Betws-y-Coed is a thriving village with a strong sense of community, boasting a range of amenities and services for visitors and residents alike. Its charming architecture and picturesque landscapes have attracted filmmakers, with movies such as "Clash of the Titans" and "First Knight" being shot on location here.

In conclusion, Betws-y-Coed is a delightful destination for anyone seeking a unique glimpse of Snowdonia's stunning landscape and rich cultural heritage. Whether you're in search of outdoor adventures, artistic inspiration, or a taste of local life, this enchanting village is not to be missed.

Broughton

Broughton, nestled in the picturesque county of Oxfordshire, is a haven of all things quaint and charming about English countryside living. Life at Broughton revolves around traditional values, and its rich historical past seeps into every aspect of life in the village. The village's historical roots are over a thousand years old and are steeped in farming, trade, and commerce. The heart of the village beats in Broughton's market square, which has been the bustling hub of merchants and traders for centuries. Historical events such as the English civil war have marked the village's past, and it has been frequented by historical figures such as Sir Winston Churchill.

Broughton's key landmarks and geographical features contribute significantly to its charm and character. Picturesque buildings exuding timeless elegance surround its market square, which has been the setting of countless village festivities. The 12th century parish church of St. Mary the Virgin, another of its architectural treasures, is a must-see for history buffs and those interested in exploring the village's religious heritage. Broughton's natural beauty also draws visitors. A walk along the banks of the River Cherwell and a visit to the nearby Blenheim Palace, a UNESCO World Heritage Site, are some of the activities visitors can indulge in.

Broughton's community takes its traditions and community spirit seriously, and the village celebrates several events and festivals, especially the Broughton Midsummer Festival, which is an explosion of colors, dance, and music. The village's local businesses, particularly the farm shop with its locally-sourced produce and crafts, are unique and add to Broughton's attraction. The village welcomes new developments while preserving its natural landscape and is a thriving community that enjoys organized events and activities that bring residents closer.

Broughton is a must-visit destination for those looking to experience quintessential English countryside life, and its historical market square, traditional festivals, and unique local businesses, all add to its charm. Visitors to Broughton leave enchanted and wanting more, relishing the opportunity to experience life back in time.

Cartmel

Discover the medieval magic of Cartmel, a delightful village nestled in the breathtaking Lake District National Park. Cobbled streets wind their way through this charming village, still steeped in old-world charm yet offering modern amenities and attractions for visitors of all ages.

One of the village's most notable landmarks is the Cartmel Priory, an architectural masterpiece of elegant stained glass windows and intricate stonework that has played a significant role in the religious and social history of the area. It has been visited by historical figures such as King Henry VIII's chief minister, Thomas Cromwell, and continues to be a must-visit for anyone interested in medieval history and stunning architecture.

Cartmel is also well known for its culinary delights, particularly its delectable sticky toffee pudding, which draws foodies from around the world to the Cartmel Village Shop. Visitors can also explore local breweries like the Unsworth's Yard Brewery and sample the cheeses at the Cartmel Cheeses shop.

Beyond food and history, Cartmel hosts a range of unique traditions and events throughout the year. From the Cartmel Agricultural Show and the Cartmel Races to exploring the natural surroundings of the Lake District National Park, visitors have plenty of ways to immerse themselves in village life.

As you meander through Cartmel, it's easy to see why it's considered one of the most special places in the UK. Its rich history, unique traditions, and picturesque setting have woven together to create a vibrant and welcoming community that will leave a lasting impression.

Chipping Campden

Nestled in the picturesque Cotswolds region of England lies the enchanting village of Chipping Campden. As you wander through its streets, it's hard not to feel transported back in time as you take in the village's rich heritage and historic charm. From its bustling market town days to its modern-day community spirit, Chipping Campden has it all.

Once a thriving wool trade center, Chipping Campden's wealth is evident in the impressive houses and public buildings dotted throughout the village. The Almshouses, Woolstaplers' Hall, and Market Hall still stand as an ode to the merchants and craftspeople who once called Campden home.

But it's not just Chipping Campden's historic past that draws visitors. The village boasts an array of cultural sites, including the stunning St. James' Church, with its exquisite stained-glass windows and mesmerizing alabaster monuments.

The Market Hall offers sanctuary and shelter to traders and visitors alike, while the Court Barn Museum showcases a wide range of traditional and contemporary crafts, including spinning, weaving, and embroidery.

Chipping Campden's natural beauty is just as impressive, with the surrounding Cotswolds Area of Outstanding Natural Beauty providing the perfect backdrop. Explore the area on foot, following the Cotswold Way as it winds its way through the village and beyond.

Despite its quaint size, Chipping Campden has a thriving community spirit that permeates throughout the village. Support local businesses such as the Campden Coffee Company, where you can enjoy delicious homemade cakes and coffee while soaking up the charming atmosphere.

With cultural events such as the Chipping Campden Literature Festival and the Campden Music Festival, it's easy to see why this village remains a beloved destination for locals and visitors alike. Chipping Campden is a must-visit for anyone seeking an authentic taste of England and a glimpse into the past that shaped this fascinating village. It's no wonder it has found its way into the pages of "100 Random Villages in the UK."

Denton

Nestled in the heart of the English countryside lies the quaint village of Denton - a place that has the power to captivate anyone who visits. From its timeless architecture steeped in history to its stunning natural surroundings, it's easy to see why Denton has secured a place in the remarkable book "100 Random Villages in the UK." In this article, we'll explore the facets of this idyllic village that make it a quintessentially British destination.

Having roots that span back to the Domesday Book of 1086, Denton is a village steeped in rich history. Its success as an agricultural village is recorded in this book, and over the centuries, it has been home to a number of notable figures, including Sir John de Creke and the 16th-century playwright, John Lyly. During the Second World War, Denton played an important role in the Royal Air Force, with many soldiers and pilots stationed there. Present-day Denton still reflects its roots through its traditional thatched cottages, winding lanes, and old-style architecture.

Visitors will find a plethora of landmarks whilst wandering through Denton. The village's local church, St. Mary's, is a superb example of Gothic architecture, with a rich history that dates back over 800 years. Meanwhile, Denton Hall - a Grade II-listed building - has been the residence of the de Creke family for five centuries. The River Waveney, which graces through the village, offers stunning views and serves as a popular destination for boating and fishing enthusiasts.

Denton's traditions and community activities exemplify the true spirit of British living. Residents of the village are immensely proud of their community spirit and unique traditions. Their Denton Carnival is a popular event where residents, visitors, and the wider community come together to celebrate the village. Additionally, the village hosts several other annual events, including music festivals, a Christmas fair, and a bi-annual scarecrow competition. Local businesses such as the Denton Deli and Bakery, The Green Dragon Inn, and the Denton Saddlery have been staples in the village, providing residents and visitors with traditional village life experiences.

Denton's picturesque surrounds and landscape could be the envy of any English village. Rolling green hills, verdant forests, and pristine heaths provide outdoor enthusiasts with ample opportunities to explore and discover the natural beauty abound. Whether hiking, cycling, or simply strolling through the fields - Denton's natural beauty is bound to leave visitors feeling revitalized and refreshed.

Eynsford

Nestled in Kent, the delightful village of Eynsford enchants visitors with its rich history and idyllic riverfront location. This hidden gem has something to offer everyone, from captivating landmarks to outdoor pursuits, traditional festivals, thriving local businesses, and a warm, welcoming community.

One of the most prominent landmarks is Eynsford Castle, a medieval masterpiece that once housed Henry VIII and Anne Boleyn. Its impressive ruins and unique design mesmerize history buffs and curious travelers alike. Another wonder is St Martin's Church, a magnificent Norman structure adorned with stunning stained-glass windows, a beautifully crafted chancel, and a 500-year-old oak door. The monumental tower, erected in the 15th century, is a sight to behold.

Equally captivating are the geographical features of Eynsford, particularly the River Darent that meanders through the village's heart. It's a hub of outdoor adventures, including fishing, kayaking, and picnicking, offering breathtaking vistas that soothe the soul.

Apart from the landmarks and natural beauty, Eynsford celebrates its heritage and tight-knit community through the annual "Hop-picking Festival." It's a vibrant showcase of the local hop-picking culture and industry, featuring traditional delicacies, local beer, and exciting games and competitions. The affable locals welcome visitors with open arms, making it a memorable experience.

If you're looking to sample the local cuisine, Eynsford has plenty of cozy pubs, quaint cafes, and restaurants serving delicious meals. The Kentish ale brewed at the local brewery is a must-try for beer lovers.

Despite its historical roots, Eynsford balances the old-world charm with modern-day amenities. It's a peaceful place to call home, with a blend of rural serenity and urban convenience that caters to all tastes. It's no wonder that Eynsford is a beloved village that draws visitors and new residents alike. Come and discover the charm of this picturesque village for yourself.

Grindleford

Nestled in the heart of the Peak District, Grindleford Village offers visitors a glimpse into the rich and fascinating history of the area. From its industrial past to its stunning natural surroundings, this small village has something to offer everyone.

The village's connection to the Peak District's industrial landscape dates back to the late 18th century when its lead mining industry attracted many who were in search of employment. Grindleford boasts notable figures such as John Farey, a geologist and surveyor, and Samuel Fox, an inventor who revolutionised the umbrella industry with his Paragon umbrella frame.

Grindleford Station, a beautifully preserved Victorian-era train station, is a prominent landmark and served as a significant transport hub for goods and people in the village's heyday. Today, it's a popular stop for walkers and hikers looking to explore the area.

Padley Chapel, a 15th-century chapel located in the surrounding countryside, provides historical and religious significance to the area. Many believe it was used by Catholic priests during the Reformation.

Picture-perfect views of the River Derwent attract visitors who want to take leisurely walks along the riverbank or relax with a picnic among the stunning natural scenery. The area is also a paradise for outdoor enthusiasts, with opportunities for hiking, cycling, and rock climbing in the dramatic gritstone edges and rolling hills.

Despite its rich past, Grindleford holds tight to its sense of community spirit. The annual Grindleford Goat Fell Race brings locals and visitors together to celebrate the village's heritage and natural beauty, while businesses such as the Sir William Hotel and Grindleford Café provide visitors with a warm welcome and the chance to experience local life.

Without a doubt, Grindleford is a village that has something for everyone. Visitors can revel in its fascinating history, explore unique landmarks, and immerse themselves in stunning natural surroundings. Meanwhile, its friendly locals and community spirit make it a charming place to call home.

Harome

Nestled in the heart of North Yorkshire Moors sits the enchanting Harome, a picturesque village that embodies all the charm and tranquility of the English countryside. It's a place where the beauty of nature meets the rich history of medieval times, and where locals have nurtured a thriving community that welcomes visitors with open arms.

Since its inception, Harome has been steeped in agriculture and farming, serving as an important stopover point for travelers on their way to the coast. Over time, this quaint village evolved into a bustling hub for trade and commerce, attracting tourists from far and wide in search of a peaceful escape.

Perhaps the most notable attraction in Harome is The Star Inn, a Michelin-starred restaurant that boasts a menu as innovative and exquisite as its service. Established in the 14th century, this iconic establishment has earned a reputation as a must-visit destination for food enthusiasts from all corners of the globe. Another icon of the village is St. Saviour's Church, a magnificent medieval church adorned with intricate stonework carefully cared for throughout centuries.

The natural beauty of Harome is equally impressive, with rolling green hills and meandering streams surrounding the village, offering a stunning backdrop for gentle hikes and camping festivities. Being located by the North York Moors National Park, it is an excellent launchpad to explore its pristine landscapes and abundant wildlife.

But what truly sets Harome apart is its thriving community spirit, with locals coming together to celebrate various events and traditions all year round. From the popular Harome scarecrow trail, where charming scarecrows line the village streets, to exploring the independently-owned shops tucked away where anything from antiques to locally grown goods and handcrafted wares offer a unique shopping experience; Harome is a place teeming with life and history, worth a visit.

Overall, Harome offers an unforgettable experience brimming with wonder, heritage, and culture. Whether you're seeking a refreshing country getaway or an opportunity to learn about a unique village with an enchanting story of its own, Harome is undoubtedly the destination to be.

Ingleton

Nestled in the heart of North Yorkshire, England, lies the quaint and charming village of Ingleton. Steeped in history, this idyllic locale is home to world-renowned sites such as the stunning waterfalls trail that draws travelers from all corners of the world. The trail is not only a representation of the village's rich history but also its geological significance.

Dating back to Viking times, Ingleton boasts a fascinating past, with records that date as far back as the Domesday Book from 1086. The village has played host to many notable figures such as the Earl of Derby, who owned the exquisite land on which the waterfalls trail is situated. Adorned with remnants of its former mining industry, the village landscape's rustic charm is a testament to its rich cultural heritage.

For centuries, the waterfalls trail has been the crown jewel of Ingleton's attractions. Visitors are transported on an enchanting journey through ancient rock formations, cascading waterfalls, and verdant greenery. The trail's geological significance, born from the limestone-rich area, is evident in the intricate rock formations that have been carved by the elements over the years, creating a mesmerizing natural wonder.

In addition to the waterfalls trail, Ingleton boasts numerous cultural sites and landmarks, including one of the oldest churches in the region, dating back to the 12th century, its bells weighing amongst the heaviest in the area. Also, among the village's gems is White Scar Cave and the Ribblehead Viaduct, both possessing fascinating geological formations known to pique interest among the curious.

Ingleton's community is tightly-knit, with local traditions that add to the village's unique charm. One such custom is its annual May Day parade, a vibrant celebration of spring that brings locals and visitors together. The delightful local business scene, which includes cozy cafes, quaint shops, and delectable restaurants, caters to both tourists and locals alike.

Surrounded by rolling hills and stunning landscapes, Ingleton provides an unbeatable destination for those who love the outdoors. Located close to the treasured Yorkshire Dales National Park renowned for its natural beauty and hiking trails, visitors will have a choice of outdoor pursuits to choose from.

Overall, Ingleton is a captivating place to visit or call home. With its extraordinary geological features and rich history, it's the quintessential destination for anyone interested in travel and culture. The village's friendly community and nature's beauty make it an irresistible, popular destination in the UK.

Kersey

Welcome to Kersey, an idyllic village that captures the true essence of medieval life in the UK. Nestled in the rolling hills of Suffolk, Kersey is a treasure trove of historical landmarks and charming community traditions that will transport you back in time.

From its rich history dating back to the 14th century to its captivating natural surroundings, Kersey has something for everyone. This village was once a bustling center for wool production, attracting merchants from across Europe, and bearing witness to the Peasants' Revolt in 1381. Today, it's a popular destination for history enthusiasts, naturalists and travelers seeking a peaceful escape.

As you explore this enchanting village, you'll discover its hidden gems, such as the well-preserved ford, which sits at the heart of the village, the stunning Gothic architecture of St. Mary's Church, and the winding lanes featuring half-timbered houses and picturesque gardens.

Kersey is more than just a beautiful village; it has a strong sense of community spirit. Locals celebrate annual events such as fairs, markets, and agricultural shows, contributing to the area's vibrant cultural heritage. Small businesses, including a 16th-century pub and a village store, add to the charm of Kersey and provide a sustaining source of locally sourced produce and crafts.

Beyond the village's limits, you'll find a breathtaking natural setting. The rolling hills, green fields, and tranquil forests provide endless opportunities for leisurely walks, hiking trails, cycling, and other outdoor pursuits.

Despite its strong historical roots, Kersey has embraced modern-day living, making it an ideal place to spend a few nights while enjoying the village's peaceful surrounds. Visitors can experience the community spirit for themselves and take part in a range of activities and events.

Overall, Kersey is a true gem that deserves to be discovered. It offers a glimpse into medieval life in the UK, as well as a peaceful escape from the hustle and bustle of modern life. So why not come and experience everything that Kersey has to offer?

Llanberis

Nestled in the heart of Snowdonia National Park, Llanberis is a true gem offering visitors a rare glimpse into the beauty and history of Wales. From its historic slate quarries to its breathtaking landscapes, this charming Welsh village boasts a rich heritage and a vibrant community that make it an unforgettable destination. Whether you're a history enthusiast, an outdoor adventurer, or simply seeking a peaceful retreat, Llanberis has something to offer.

The village's roots go back to Roman times, with Saint Peris said to have founded a monastic cell in the area. Llanberis rose to prominence during the 19th century slate industry boom, producing some of the finest roofing materials, gravestones, and even snooker tables. But the village is more than just its industrial history. Its key landmarks include the Snowdon Mountain Railway, which offers breathtaking views of Mount Snowdon, and the National Slate Museum that showcases the area's rich mining heritage.

Natural beauty abounds in Llanberis, with Llyn Padarn, a picturesque lake that is a popular spot for fishing, kayaking, and wild swimming. For those looking for a more challenging adventure, the area's hiking and walking trails offer stunning views of the mountains and countryside. But what makes Llanberis truly special is its community spirit, with events such as the Snowdonia Marathon and the Llanberis Food Festival that bring locals and visitors together.

Llanberis has seen many modern developments in recent years, including the Llanberis Adventure Centre that offers a range of outdoor activities and a cycle path that runs along the shores of Llyn Padarn. Despite these developments, the village has managed to maintain its unique character and charm, ensuring that visitors and residents alike continue to experience the magic of this special place.

In conclusion, Llanberis is much more than a gateway to Snowdonia National Park. It is a living testament to the rich history, unique traditions, and vibrant community of Wales. Whether you're exploring its cultural landmarks, enjoying its natural beauty, or simply soaking up its friendly atmosphere, Llanberis is sure to leave a lasting impression.

Middleton-in-Teesdale

As you enter Middleton-in-Teesdale, you'll feel as if you've been transported to another time and place. This charming village nestled in the heart of the Durham Dales is steeped in history and natural beauty. As part of our "100 Random Villages in the UK" series, we're excited to take you on a journey to discover the many treasures of this quaint location.

Middleton-in-Teesdale has a long and rich history dating all the way back to the Roman period when it played a crucial role as a crossing point of the Tees. But it was during the 19th century that the village truly flourished, serving as the hub of the lead mining industry in the region. This newfound wealth allowed for the construction of many of the village's notable structures, including the stately Town Hall and the stunning St. Mary's Church.

One of the village's most notable figures is Henry Hopper, who played a crucial role in bringing the first railway to the area. Thanks to his efforts, Middleton-in-Teesdale was connected to larger cities, paving the way for new possibilities for trade and commerce in the region.

One of Middleton-in-Teesdale's most striking features is its architecture. The grand Town Hall, completed in 1862, still serves as a hub for community events, and St. Mary's Church, with its stone walls and exquisite Norman detailing, has stood proudly since the 12th century. These impressive structures are perfect examples of the village's cultural heritage.

But it's not just the architecture that impresses; Middleton-in-Teesdale is also known for its natural beauty. The River Tees winds its way through the village, providing endless opportunities for outdoor recreation, from fishing to kayaking and swimming. A short drive from the village, visitors can marvel at the breathtaking waterfalls at Low Force and High Force.

The village has a strong sense of community spirit that's evident in its many local traditions. Events like the annual Agricultural Show and the Christmas Market offer a taste of the village's vibrant culture. Middleton-in-Teesdale also boasts a thriving business community, with local craft shops, cafes, and restaurants offering unique products and experiences that are hard to find elsewhere.

In short, Middleton-in-Teesdale is a captivating and welcoming destination that has something to offer everyone, from history buffs to nature lovers and everyone in between. Whether you're stopping in for a visit or planning to call it home, you'll marvel at the charm and beauty of this quintessential British village.

Niton

Nestled along the stunning southern coast of the Isle of Wight, Niton is one of the many hidden gems waiting to be discovered in the UK. With its unique landscape and rich history, this picturesque village boasts a character like no other.

At the core of Niton's identity stands the Niton Lighthouse, an iconic landmark that has stood tall for over 150 years. Set on the edge of Niton Undercliff, this scenic area is a drawcard for adventurers and nature lovers. With remarkable landslips and a unique ecology, Niton Undercliff is a site of great scientific interest.

Niton's history can be traced back to the Anglo-Saxon period, with the village retaining much of its past to this day. Notable historical figures, like Sir John Harrington, who installed the first flushing toilet in an English house, have called Niton home, contributing to the village's development.

Local residents take pride in their heritage, as evidenced by Niton's vibrant community spirit. The annual carnival, held every August, is a standout event, bringing together locals and visitors alike for a day of fun and games. The Niton Village Market is another community highlight, with residents showcasing their crafts and produce.

For outdoor enthusiasts, Niton is a paradise with an abundance of scenic walks, breathtaking views of the coast, and the opportunity to explore Niton Undercliff's unique ecology and geology. It's the ideal destination for those interested in cultural exploration and travel.

All in all, Niton is a must-visit destination that has maintained its charm and authenticity. It's one of the 100 random villages that should be on everyone's bucket list.

Orford

Nestled within the stunning landscape of Suffolk coastal heathland lies the charming village of Orford, celebrated for its history, natural beauty, and traditional charm. The village is situated at the mouth of the River Ore on the east coast of England and boasts a unique and fascinating history.

Orford Ness, an area of outstanding natural beauty, has played a vital role throughout history. It served as a military site during the Napoleonic Wars and was later used as a testing ground for weapons during World War II. Today, it is a nature reserve that is home to a diverse range of bird species, making it a significant site for bird-watchers.

The village's most notable landmark is the magnificent Orford Castle. Built in the 12th century by Henry II, the fortress played a pivotal role in defending the region against French invasion during the medieval period. Today, it remains a popular tourist attraction and is open to the public for exploration.

Orford Museum is another cultural highlight that showcases the rich history of the village and surrounding area. Its exhibits, which include prehistoric bones and Roman pottery, give visitors a glimpse into the fascinating past of this unique destination.

Orford is also renowned for its unique traditions and community activities that are enjoyed by both locals and tourists. The annual Orford Flower Show is a much-anticipated event that draws crowds from across the country. Additionally, the village boasts a range of quaint boutique shops and traditional pubs that contribute to the character and charm of the area.

The natural surroundings of Orford will take your breath away, with its stunning coastal heathland and beautiful estuary. Hike through the sand dunes, take a boat trip to explore the local wildlife or visit the Orford Ness nature reserve for a chance to spot migratory birds and other fascinating wildlife.

Finally, the village's community spirit and modern amenities make Orford an attractive place to visit or live. Despite being a relatively small village, it boasts excellent facilities, including a primary school, post office, and medical practice. The friendly locals and the range of events and activities on offer throughout the year only add to its charm.

In conclusion, Orford is a truly unique and special destination that offers a fascinating glimpse into the cultural and natural beauty of the UK. Its rich history, stunning natural surroundings, and friendly community make it an unmissable destination.

Printed in Great Britain
by Amazon